RESURGENCE OF ORGANICISM

edited by Sarah Bonnemaison

with contributions from

Philip Beesley
Carole Collet
Brian Lilley
Alan Macy
Steven Mannell
Jenny Sabin

and graduate architecture students
from Dalhousie University

Riverside Architectural Press | Dalhousie Architectural Press

Publisher:
Riverside Architectural Press in collaboration with Dalhousie Architectural Press
www.riversidearchitecturalpress.ca
www.dal.ca/archpress

Publication design, editing, layout and production:
Christine Macy

Copy editing:
Susanne Marshall

Library and Archives Canada Cataloguing in Publication

Title: Resurgence of Organicism / edited by Sarah Bonnemaison.
Names: Bonnemaison, Sarah, 1958- editor. | Living Architecture Systems Group, issuing body.

Description: Catalogue of an exhibition held at the Living Architecture Systems Group Symposium from March 1 to 3, 2019, in Toronto, Ontario. | Contributions by Philip Beesley, Carole Collet, Brian Lilley, Alan Macy, Steven Mannell, Jenny Sabin, and graduate students from Dalhousie University, School of Architecture.

Identifiers: Canadiana 20190061170 | ISBN 9781988366203 (paperback)
Subjects: LCSH: Architecture, Modern—21st century—Exhibitions. | LCSH: Nature (Aesthetics)—Exhibitions. | LCSH: Organicism (Philosophy)—Exhibitions. | LCSH: Art and architecture—Exhibitions. | LCGFT: Exhibition catalogs.
Classification: LCC NA687.R47 2019 | DDC 720.1/08—dc23

This book is set in Zurich Lt BT and Garamond

Front cover: Rendering of Lumen, Jenny Sabin Studio for MoMA and MoMA PS1 YAP 2017

A NOTE ON THE EXHIBITION CATALOGUE

The exhibition "Resurgence of Organicism" originated as a graduate seminar taught by Sarah Bonnemaison at Dalhousie University's School of Architecture. In Fall 2018, graduate architecture students investigated the history and theory of organicism—through a close reading of Caroline van Eck's seminal book on the topic—to understand its architectural manifestations over the course of centuries, and created an exhibition and catalogue.

On the occasion of the Living Architecture Systems Group symposium in Spring 2019, Bonnemaison redesigned the exhibition to adapt to a new venue at OCAD University in Toronto. The catalogue has been expanded to include contributions from contemporary architects and artists who share their own quest for bio-design, showing us how nature is, more than ever, a source of inspiration for the designer.

CONTENTS

Zaha Hadid, Afragola Station, Naples, 2017

RESURGENCE OF ORGANICISM
Sarah Bonnemaison

In this exhibition we share the results of ongoing research into "living architecture." This research traces its roots back to the philosophy of "organicism," the art of learning from nature to create beautiful architecture. Indeed, the close connection between living nature and architecture is one of the most persistent and enduring themes of architectural theory. In the West it has come to be called organicism.

For the creator, organicism can be seen as strategies of both invention and interpretation that draw from nature. The strategy of invention operates through a deep understanding of living nature. The strategy of interpretation is based on the belief that the whole is larger than its parts.

In the sciences, organicism is a

> materialistic philosophy where complex wholes are inherently greater than the sum of their parts in the sense that the properties of each part are dependent upon the context of the part within the whole in which they operate. Thus, when we try to explain how the whole system behaves, we have to talk about the context of the whole and cannot get away talking only about the parts.[1]

Reaching out to the natural sciences continues a well-established tradition of architects who learned from biologist D'Arcy Thompson about the growth structure of skeletons and geometrical patterns in plants.[2] In this worldview, the organic is interpreted with stone carvings, wood curves, and colored glass, to give the illusion of living nature.

Organicism was renamed "organic," and Frank Lloyd Wright became its main proponent. But the working methods actually came from older forms of organicism. For example, Wright used the seed as a form generator. The geometries repeat at different scales, from small window decorations to large supporting columns, thereby creating a harmonious whole. Le Corbusier developed the modulor based on Fibonacci series, and Christopher Alexander created a pattern language. Frei Otto invented an aesthetics for modern tents using soap film models, Pier Luigi Nervi and Felix Candela built thin double curved surfaces in concrete, Santiago

Calatrava created metal arches inspired by animal bones, and, more recently, Zaha Hadid designed large complex shell-like curves in metal and glass. They all pursued an organic mode of thinking.

Today we have a multitude of terms that come mostly from the sciences. Architects have attempted to respond to the development of the natural sciences by naming their practice organic, ecological, green, zoomorphic and, more recently, creating robotic structures based on biomimicry. All this in a context of serious ecological crisis. The philosophy of organicism offers a large palette of ideas, methods and practices that can enrich our conversations and fuel creation. Contemporary digital technologies and robotics can help us go beyond simple mimicry of nature, providing opportunities for greater complexity and depth. The magic lies in the hands of the designer who can, at last, reconnect with our ancient yearning to dwell in living nature.

This exhibition makes explicit design methods that are drawn from living nature, and draws links between buildings across centuries and countries into five constellations. One could draw other links between these particular buildings but today we chose themes drawn from the philosphy of organicism that we see repeatedly. These themes are:

I.   Growth from Within
II. Harmonic Unity
III. Macrocosm and Microcosm
IV. Geometries Derived from Nature
V.   The Human Body as a Metaphor of Nature

Two major events generated a radical turn in organicism. The first occurred in 1543 when Copernicus argued that the sun was at the centre and the earth was rotating around it. The second was the photograph of the earth taken from the moon in 1968, which triggered an ecological response that is still with us today.

As we look back at the architectural canon, some works seem to float up above the others in the way they beautifully express our relationship to nature, whether through their use of geometry or their materials. Each essay that follows interprets a unique aspect of organicism and puts it in its proper theoretical context. The catalogue, along with the exhibition, reveals the enduring strength of organicism in architectural education, research, and practice. The influence of Gottfried Semper, for example, on the teaching of technology and wall assembly is one among many.

Perhaps the most enduring aspect of organicism is its potential, as a theory, to put into words the explorations, interpretations and creation of new forms, new ways to assemble, and new building materials. When in doubt, we seem to always return to nature, whether it be for its spiritual power, or for its infinite source of inspiration.

---

1 Scott Gilbert. "Embracing Complexity: Organicism for the 21st Century." *Developmental Dynamics 219* (2000): 1-9.
2 D'Arcy Wentworth Thompson, *On Growth and Form*. Cambridge: Cambridge University Press, 1917.

EXHIBITION THEMES - AN OVERVIEW

	ANTIQUITY	MEDIEVAL	EARLY MODERN	18-19TH CENTURY
GROWTH	Ise Grand Shrine 640 BCE Temple of Hercules Victor, 146 BCE	Angkor Wat, 1150	Walled Citadel, Serlio, 1550 San Biago, Sangallo the Elder, 1518	*Metamorphosis of Plants*, Goethe, 1790
HARMONY	Parthenon, 447 BCE	Cologne Cathedral, 1248	Sant' Andrea, Mantua, Alberti, 1471	Oxford Museum, Woodward, 1855
COSMOS	The Great Cosmic Mountain, Borobudur, 800	Silvacane Abbey, 1144	Tempietto, Bramante, 1502	Cenotaph for Newton, Boullée, 1784 Shaker Round Barn, 1826
GEOMETRY	Minaret, Great Mosque of Samarra, 851	Alhambra, 889 Notre-Dame de Paris,1163	Sheikh Lotfollah Mosque, Shaykh Bahai, 1619 Taj Mahal, 1648	Bibliothèque Ste-Geneviève, Labrouste,1850
BODY	Caryatids, Erechtheion, 5th c BCE	Cluny III Abbey, 1131	*Vitruvian Man*, Leonardo da Vinci	Chinese-style Mirror Cabinet Bayreuth Palace, Margrave Wilhemine, 1750

COPERNICAN REVOLUTION

19TH CENTURY	20TH CENTURY				21ST CENTURY
Bell Auditorium, Adler and Sullivan, 1890 Hôtel Tassel, Horta, 1894	Unity Temple, Wright, 1908 *On Growth and Form*, Thompson, 1917		Habitat, Safdie, 1967 Brion Cemetery, Scarpa,1969	Nakagin Capsule Tower, Kurokawa, 1972	Hylozoic Soil, Beesley, 2005
The Seven Lamps of Architecture, Ruskin, 1849 *Four Elements of Architecture*, Semper, 1851	Avon Old Farms, Pope Riddle, 1928 Villa Mairea, Aalto, 1938		Amsterdam Orphanage, Van Eyck, 1960	HtwoOexpo, NOX/ Lars Spuybroek, 1997	Green School, IBUKU, 2017 Chulah stoves, Lari, 2010
Marshall Field Store, Richardson, 1892 Monadnock Block, Burnham and Root, 1891	Einstein Tower, Mendelsohn, 1921	EARTH SEEN FROM SPACE	US Pavillon, Fuller, 1967	The Ark, Solsearch, 1976 Eden Project, Grimshaw, 2000	Blur Building, Diller+Scofidio, 2002 Jade Eco Park, Rahm et al, 2016
Sagrada Familia, Gaudi,1882- Paris Mêtro, Guimard, 1913	City Tower, Tyng and Kahn,1953 Ronchamp, Le Corbusier, 1955		Bridges, Le Ricolais, 1960s German Pavillon, Frei Otto, 1967	*Fractal Geometry of Nature*, Madelbrot, 1982	Burnham Pavilion, Hadid, 2009 Lumen, Sabin, 2019
Palais Stoclet, Hoffmann, 1911	E1027, Gray, 1929 Modulor, Le Corbusier, 1948 Endless House, Kiesler, 1960		Cushicle, Webb, 1964 School of Plastic Arts, Porro, 1962	Fountains, Halprin, 1970s	Gestures, Filum, 2006

I. GROWTH FROM WITHIN

The seed, and the fundamental idea of growth from within, is a design strategy that allows architecture to be conceived as part of a landscape that changes over time, according to its own internal logic. The Roman Temple of Hercules Victor and the Renaissance church of San Biagio display architectural decorum, meaning that the site and circumstances were considered the seeds for their conception. Today, the idea of decorum is described as being "integrated in the urban landscape." But the metaphor is the same — meaning that new buildings should fit in their landscapes as if they had "grown" there. Such integration is a fundamental value in organicism. The "seed" in Frank Lloyd Wright's work, for example, is the hearth, which anchors growth in the plan and generates the design of the building as a form in itself and its extension into the surrounding landscape. The concept that buildings adapt and change over time is central to this theme. We see this in the Japanese Metabolist movement, in which a structural core supports plug-in units to accommodate ever-changing human activities. To develop their organicist argument for growth and adaptation in the modern city, the Metabolists refer all the way back to the Ise Grand Shrine, which was created in 640 BC, and since then, has been entirely rebuilt every 25 years.

Ideas can also "seed" other ideas. In the early 20th century, Antonio Gaudi used hanging chains to discover the geometry of purely tensile forms — which he then inverted to model the purely compressive forms of his extraordinary Sagrada Familia cathedral in Barcelona. Contemporary architect and engineer Santiago Calatrava works with these same geometries, extending their logic to create spectacular vaulted spaces such as the Umbracle in Valencia, the Liège-Guillemins train station (2009), and the World Trade Centre Oculus in New York City (2016).

The theme of "growth from within" resurfaces beautifully in the contemporary living architectures of Philip Beesley and the Living Architecture Systems Group. In this work, light flexible fronds are the seeds sown in each installation. With each new iteration of this extended design research program, the frond changes a little — adapting to new demands, integrating robotics and sensors, and multiplying to fill a whole environment like leaves swirling in the wind.

Opposite: Santiago Calatrava, L'Umbracle, Valencia, 2001

APTNESS AS ARCHITECTURAL DECORUM
Luke Godden

For something to be apt, it must be suitable, appropriate, or fit within particular circumstances. Aptness in the realm of organicism, as described by Caroline van Eck, is one of Leon Battista Alberti's four terms to describe his conception of nature as a model for the architect. The other three terms, *concinnitas*, opposition, and variety are interlinked; concinnitas, the "unifying category," refers to the harmonious composition of opposing and varying forms. This unity, according to van Eck, "is based on its aptness for or adaptation to a purpose," for "nature, the supreme artificer, proceeds according to plan and purpose."[1] Aptness is also used by Cicero and Quintilianus in rhetorical contexts; a speech is deemed apt if appropriate to its aims, subject matter, and audience.[2] Rhetorical aptness is thus analogous to architecture, which must also suit a given purpose and audience. In this way, aptness in the realm of building is equivalent to architectural decorum.

Architectural decorum refers to the suitability of a design to its purpose and context. Surfacing in Classical architecture and prevailing as a guiding design principle from the Renaissance period until the dawn of modernity, decorum is achieved when a building's site and circumstances can be perceived as the seeds for its conception. Decorum itself has two principal aspects: functional and site decorum. Functional decorum, referring to a building's apt portrayal of its purpose, involves the use of certain materials and architectural orders to represent use, dedication, or patron status.[3] Site decorum is a strategy, often used by Italian Renaissance architects, to determine a building's appropriate volumes and detail level depending on the distance of the observer.[4] Three case studies, namely the Temple of Hercules Victor, Serlio's "Walled Citadel," and the Church of San Biagio, reveal various expressions of these two aspects of decorum, as they informed architectural theory.

Prior to modernist thought, buildings were designed to symbolize their societal purpose. Precise combinations of materials, ornament, and architectural orders revealed social status, making architecture a vehicle for exemplifying civility, social order, and national pride.[5] In ancient Rome, for example, materials were selected

Left to right: (1) Temple of Hercules Victor; (2) Detail of Temple columns

according to patron, location, monument type, material availability, and intended audience.[6] Furthermore, a Greek influence in the style and materials of Roman Republic architecture was meant to convey triumph and prestige.

Functional decorum as a strategy to convey such triumph is plainly illustrated in the Temple of Hercules Victor, a Roman temple erected after the consul Lucius Mummius achieved victory over the Greeks, conquering Corinth in 146 BC (Figure 1). The monument depicts Greece succumbing to Rome. With a clear Greek influence, the *tholos* features a peripteral form and Corinthian capitals (Figure 2). Sourced from the Greek mainland, Pentelic marble comprises the entire visible exterior, acting as a "symbolic spoil of war, broadcasting Mummius's defeat of the resplendent city of Corinth."[7] This choice of materials visually associates the monument with the source of triumph, making the Temple of Hercules Victor an apt representation of victory in ancient Rome.

Functional decorum was also employed in the appropriate selection of classical architectural orders. Sebastiano Serlio, a Bolognese author and architect of the Late Renaissance period, helped establish each order's suitability to certain building typologies. In his final (unpublished) book, Serlio uses Polybius's description of temporary Roman military camps to reconstruct what he calls a "Walled Citadel," using decorum to determine each structure's appropriate order. For instance, Serlio prescribed the Doric order for the *porta pretorea*, suitable for buildings "for men of arms" with a "delicate side" to their character.[8] Vaughan Hart adequately summarizes Serlio's logic in the selection of these orders: the city's

> public buildings are ornamented with the orders — moving from "military" Doric in the centre through the more "gentle" Ionic and Corinthian on either side to the Composite, the order of Roman "triumph," on the outermost buildings.[9]

Functional decorum is hence used here as a strategy to determine which particular order will aptly convey each building's purpose in the city structure.

Site decorum considers the physical position of the viewer relative to a given building. In particular, the design is calibrated to the observer's perspective when determining the appropriate forms and level of detail. For Italian Renaissance architects, site decorum was established through elements of scenography. This stemmed from a profound understanding of linear perspective — manipulating elements to coordinate the observer's sight-lines — and atmospheric perspective — addressing the tendency of distant objects to become obscured — which led architects to emphasize the horizontal, vertical, and massed elements of a building.[10] Accordingly, form and profile took precedence over refined detailing and ornamentation for buildings situated outside cities, which were principally viewed from afar.

Built between 1518 and 1540, the Church of San Biagio (Figure 3) effectively demonstrates site decorum. Situated in the hills outside Montepulciano in Tuscany, its architect Antonio da Sangallo the Elder devoted substantial time to considering how the church would be seen from the city. When viewed from afar, the church demonstrates that Sangallo had considered its juxtaposition with the surrounding trees and hills, as the building is "distinctive for the manner in which its cubic, cylindrical, and semi-spherical volumes can be registered at great distance, standing out against the landscape."[11] Moreover, in 1533, the heights of the dome and the tower were increased to emphasize verticality in the landscape and contrast with the cubic church body below.[12] Throughout its construction, the design of San Biagio thus became clearer and more monumental as a distant object in the landscape, emphasized by volumes and outline.

Architectural decorum has been, throughout its history, a valuable design principle for its ability to connect built form with its context. Hill and Kohane suggest however, that despite its prevalence in the Classical and Renaissance periods, "to some extent, architectural decorum is a phenomenon of the history of ideas, one that developed and declined along with the societies of which it was part."[13] As the "international style" emerged with the Industrial Revolution, so did the eclipse of architectural decorum in theory and practice, interrupting buildings' connections with their time and place. Ultimately, decorum's disuse "contributed to the perception that architecture, above all the arts, was disconnected from its society."[14] However, although not the predominant theory it once was, architectural decorum today continues to present opportunities for use — as a tool for analyzing buildings according to a given epoch — and invention — as a strategy to ensure a design expresses contextual aptness.

(3) Madonna di San Biagio, Montepulciano

1   Caroline van Eck, *Organicism in Nineteenth-Century Architecture: an Inquiry into Its Theoretical and Philosophical Background*, Amsterdam: Architectura et Natura Press, 1994, 50.
2   van Eck, *Organicism*, 51.
3   Vaughan Hart, "Decorum and the Five Orders of Architecture: Sebastiano Serlio's Military City," RES: *Anthropology and Aesthetics* 34, no. 34 (1998): 75.
4   Michael Hill and Peter Kohane, "Site Decorum," *Architectural Theory Review* 20, no. 2 (2015): 228.
5   Michael Hill and Peter Kohane, "The Eclipse of a Commonplace Idea: Decorum in Architectural Theory," *Arq: Architectural Research Quarterly* 5, no. 1 (2001): 68.
6   Maggie L. Popkin, "Decorum and the Meanings of Materials in Triumphal Architecture of Republican Rome," *Journal of the Society of Architectural Historians* 74, no. 3 (2015): 289.
7   Popkin, "Decorum and the Meanings of Materials," 296.
8   Hart, "Decorum and the Five Orders," 79.
9   Hart, "Decorum and the Five Orders," 82.
10 Hill and Kohane, "Site Decorum," 228.
11 Hill and Kohane, "Site Decorum," 230.
12 Hill and Kohane, "Site Decorum," 233.
13 Hill and Kohane, "The Eclipse of a Commonplace Idea," 73.
14 Hill and Kohane, "The Eclipse of a Commonplace Idea," 65.

BEAUTY + UNITY: THE SEED AS A DESIGN STRATEGY
Darren Fransen

The concept of the seed, and growth from within, has been a unifying design strategy throughout organicism, with some of the best examples seen in Frank Lloyd Wright's Unity Temple (1908) and his Usonian homes.

According to Leon Battista Alberti, beauty is a function of what he calls "unity," a dominant characteristic within nature which has the potential to regulate and connect contrasting elements. Unity is not based on modularity, common measurements or expressed mathematical proportions, but instead on the conceptual whole, which then determines the structure of its parts.[1] Wright's philosophy and architectural approach, similarly, use the conceptual strategy of the "seed" to regulate and connect contrasting elements through what he calls "completeness in idea and execution."[2] Where Alberti and Wright differ is in the way each relates this concept of unity to nature and organicism. Alberti suggests that unity is something pure that cannot be added to, taken away from, or altered,[3] which contrasts with the characteristic of growth found within nature. Wright, on the other hand, embraces growth as a core characteristic in his organic architecture, relying on the seed as a design strategy to maintain unity, and in turn beauty, within his architecture.

When Oak Park's Unitarian congregation lost their church to a fire in 1905, Frank Lloyd Wright — as a Unitarian and a resident of Oak Park — welcomed the opportunity to work on the commission. To express spatial and formal unity, he used the seed as a design strategy to organize the building, both linking and differentiating the two monolithic concrete forms (Figure 1). According to William Curtis, the first conceptual form and seed of the project, is the sanctuary, expressed as a classical square geometry most likely influenced by Wright's mentor Louis Sullivan.[4] Its pure geometry suggests stability, wholeness and unity, while at the same time creating a centralized focus around which the remainder of the building revolves (Figure 2). The second conceptual form, housing the Sunday school and meeting hall, can be considered subservient to the first, the "growth" from the seed. To maintain architectural clarity of idea, and the desired hierarchical

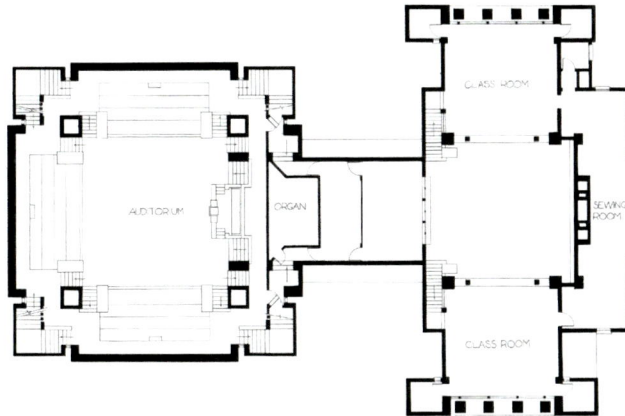

relationship, the geometry of the Sunday school was compressed into a rectangular volume. To maintain the relation between the two buildings, the cross axis of the Sunday school was centered on the sanctuary.

To further execute the design strategy, Wright elevated the experiential quality of the sanctuary by "demolishing the box," cutting away its walls and roof to achieve a sense of unrestricted space. The introduction of clerestories into the walls transform them into screens, and the piercing of skylights through the roof allow it to open up to the sky.[6] To elevate the space even further, leaded glazing filters the natural light, casting a soft warmth throughout the monolithic concrete space, connecting the classical geometry and religious iconography into a harmonious whole.[7] The composition has strong similarities with traditional Japanese tea houses, as seen in the Katsura Imperial villa (Figure 3).

The first Usonian home was constructed in Madison, Wisconsin in 1937, for Herbert and Katherine Jacobs. It also achieves unity, and in turn

Top to bottom: (1) Plan, Unity Temple; (2) Sanctuary, Unity Temple; (3) Geppa-ro Tea Pavilion, Katsura Villa, Japan

beauty, through the rhetoric of the seed. Wright organized his homes in response to the evolving American landscape and his own personal convictions; he envisioned homes as the root, or core, of the American culture, in which individuals could grow "out of the ground and into the light."[8] These homes were a response to the Great Depression, designed for middle class Americans who envisioned a new, simpler way of living that celebrated the coming together of the informal family.[9]

To achieve this sense of coming together, Wright organized the dwelling around a central core he called "the workspace," at the intersection of the two radiating wings, as can be seen in the plan (Figure 4). Here are the kitchen and laundry. The seeds of the Usonian homes are their masonry cores, used to separate active spaces like the living room from the quiet bedroom spaces.[10] Wright also created a hierarchy of materials that reinforced his conceptual design strategy: the core as a conceptual seed is rendered as a brick mass to magnify its presence. The walls facing the garden are conceptually removed, rendered with glass to connect the occupant with nature (Figure 5). The rest of the home is clad in wood, to achieve privacy while at the same time supporting the masonry core as a unifying element.

The concept of the seed, and growth from within, is used throughout architectural discourse as a unifying, and therefore beautifying, strategy. This design strategy allowed Wright to achieve a natural sense of growth in his architecture, placing a unifying element at the heart of each building, around which the remainder of the space radiates. Wright's unifying elements are always elevated — through the use of geometry, light, or materiality — to express their generative power, as seen in the Unity Temple and Usonian homes. Frank Lloyd Wright continues this design strategy throughout his work, from the early projects such as the Robie House, to later works such as the Guggenheim Museum and Johnson Wax headquarters.

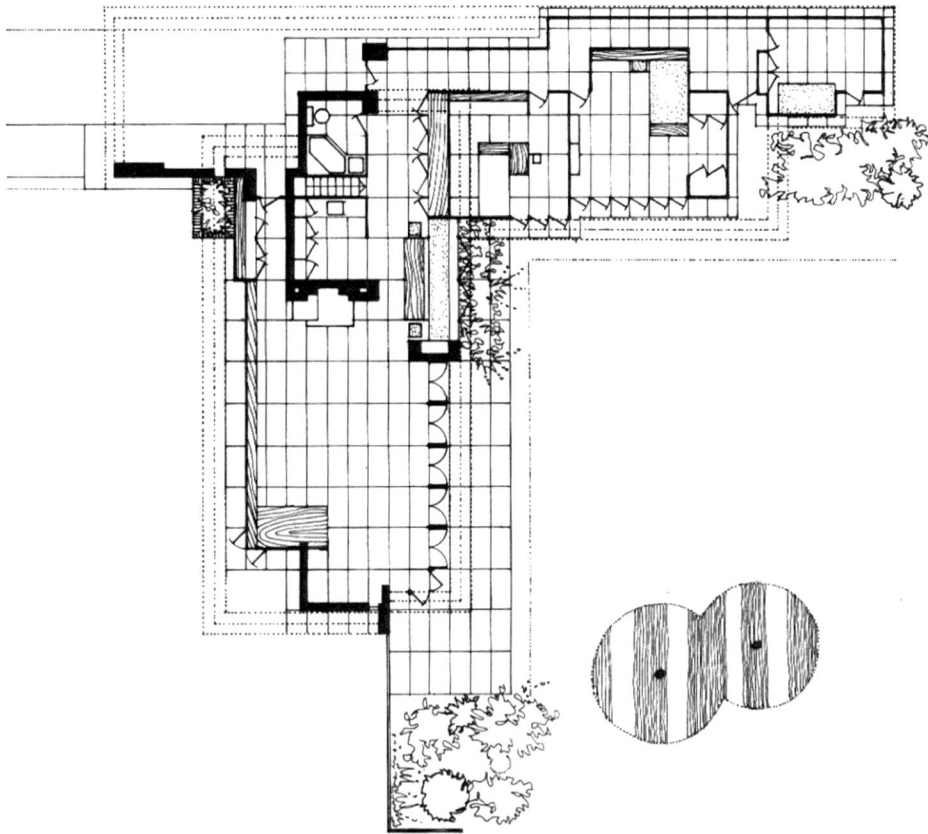

Above: (4) Plan, Jacobs House
Opposite page: (5) Courtyard view, Jacobs House

1   Caroline van Eck, *Organicism in Nineteenth-century Architecture: An Inquiry into Its Theoretical and Philosophical Background*. Amsterdam: Architectura et Nature Press, 1994, 48.
2   Frank Lloyd Wright and Patrick Joseph Meehan, *Truth against the World: Frank Lloyd Wright Speaks for an Organic Architecture*. New York: Wiley, 1987, 51.
3   van Eck, *Organicism,* 52.
4   William J.R. Curtis, *Modern Architecture since 1900* (3rd ed.), Upper Saddle River, NJ: Prentice Hall, 1996, 128.
5   Curtis, *Modern Architecture*, 127.
6   Wright and Meehan, *Truth against the World*, 287.
7   "Unity Temple," *Frank Lloyd Wright Trust*. Accessed October 29, 2018. https://flwright.org/researchexplore/unitytemple.
8   John Sergeant, *Frank Lloyd Wright's Usonian Houses: The Case for Organic Architecture*. New York: Whitney Library of Design, 1976,16.
9   Sergeant, *Wright's Usonian Houses*, 14.
10 William Allin Storrer and Frank Lloyd Wright, *The Architecture of Frank Lloyd Wright: a Complete Catalog* (2d ed.) Cambridge, MA: MIT Press, 1978, 234.

JAPANESE METABOLISM:
A SYNTHESIS OF TRADITION AND MODERNISM
Bilal Khan

In the 1950s, in the midst of Japan's post-war economic boom, a group of Japanese architects led by Kenzo Tange formed a group known as the "Metabolists." They presented their ideas at the 1960 World Design Conference in Tokyo, proposing an alternative to the prevailing wave of development; this event placed Metabolism on the world stage.[1] Metabolist discourses are rooted in Japanese culture and particularly the Shinto religion, in their emphasis on change, regeneration, and growth. In this sense, Metabolist architecture aligns with organicism.

An early word used for Metabolism was *shinchintaisha*, generally defined as "regeneration," "renewal," and "metabolism."[2] This cluster of associations paradoxically denotes both construction and deconstruction. For Metabolists, this paradox embodies the essence of "Japanese-ness," a unique element of which was seen to be the capability to regain a sense of space and place after cyclical conditions of *tabula rasa*.[3]

This paradox is demonstrated in the ancient Shinto tradition of cyclical regeneration, involving the partial or total dismantling of the frames of sacred buildings and their reconstruction on a new site (Figure 1). Ise Grand Shrine is one of the most celebrated examples of this ritual of impermanence.[4] As Rem Koolhaas puts it, "Japanese people do not hold on to things"[5] — there is a strong Japanese tradition of making buildings and cities impermanent. Japanese culture recognizes the permanence of "life spirit," and therefore has no need for permanent structures to symbolize permanence. This notion contrasts with Western associations of permanence with monumentality. In a Japanese approach, material is merely an expression of the "essence of life," not an end in itself.[6]

Kawazoe Noboru elaborates, explaining that the Japanese value the spirit rather than the actual structure, and concludes that Ise Shrine, "ever new, yet ever unchanging," reverses the Western dictum "life is short, art eternal."[7] The idea of Ise as "autochthonous, primordial, and self-renewing" inspired Kawazoe and the Japanese architects of his generation.[8]

Left to right: (1) Aerial view of Ise Shrine, showing old shrine and new; (2) *Onbashira* wooden post, Suwa Grand Shrine complex, Nagano prefecture; (3) Horikawa Space Capsule toy, 1960s

Closely associated with the dismantling of the structure of the Ise Shrine is the "placement of the pillar" ritual, a space-forming architectural element that symbolizes a sense of "rooted-ness" to a specific place.[9] The symbolic pillar takes a functional role in Metabolist architecture in the form of structural core (Figure 2).[10]

The other basic unit of Metabolism is the capsule (Figure 3).[11] The fusion of core and capsule forms the focus of Metabolist architecture, where the structural core is used as the building's "spinal column" and as the principal component of a spatial scaffolding (an aggregation of capsules) on an urban scale. The core has a double identity as an archetypal form and as a sophisticated technological device.[12]

In Kiyonori Kikutake's "Tower City" project of 1958 (Figure 4), prefabricated steel housing units are envisioned suspended from a hollow, cylindrical, 300-meter high structural core. The design anticipates growth — from the original scheme of 1,500 dwellings for 5,000 residents, the structural cores could be extended, and more units added. While each structural core was imagined to be durable, the life span of the dwellings was set at fifty years, and the overall configuration of the building would not be affected by the changes brought about by growth or decay.[13]

This precept of Metabolist architecture can be understood through Bötticher's concept of natural organisms growing outward from a seed.[14] In this case, the structural core of the building can be seen as the seed, allowing growth as each capsule is added; through aggregation, the structure grows organically. The structural core, extrapolating Bötticher's concept, can be interpreted as the tectonic concept.[15] Similarly, Goethe's metaphor of a leaf clearly articulates the relationship of a capsule to the structural core, as he believed that all the advanced parts of a plant (the building) were variations from one seminal element, the leaf (the capsule), and all advanced parts of the plant could be regarded as "transformations of one, single basic organ."[16]

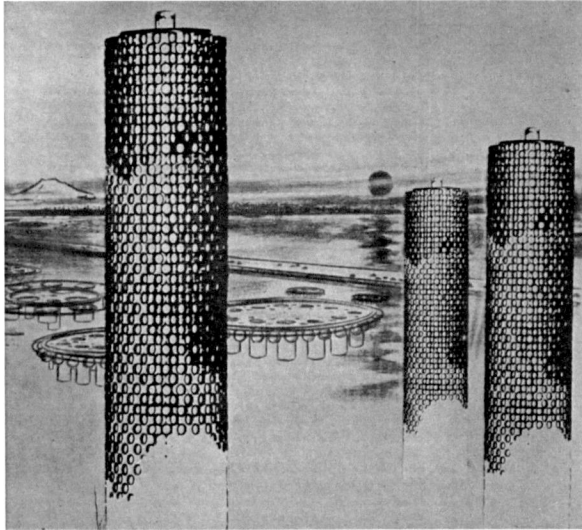

(4) Kiyonori Kikutake, Tower City

These concepts are further synthesized in Kisho Kurokawa's Nakagin Tower from 1970 (Figure 5). The world's first capsule building, it is comprised of two massive circulation towers supporting 144 capsules, which are plugged in like branches and leaves on a tree trunk.[17] Each capsule, attached to the tower with four high-tension bolts, is designed to accommodate individuals, in the form of an apartment or a studio space (Figure 6). Connecting units can also accommodate a family.[18]

Another project, Kurokawa's experimental "Helix City" from 1961, shows the relationship of the tower to supporting units quite literally, where the structural core is used for circulation of people and services, and the capsules are nestled like leaves on branches attached to the core. These examples clearly suggest that as the Metabolists' structural core developed from its grounding in Shinto tradition, its ritualistic identity and mechanistic role have been preserved as fixed points of reference within Metabolist practice.

Gottfried Semper's writings shed light on the similarities between nature and Metabolist practices: "works of nature and creations by humans are connected with each other by a few fundamental thoughts, which have found their simplest expression in some original forms or types."[19] Natural phenomenon have indeed been embodied in the works of Metabolists, as matters of functional importance, tied to the ritual of place-making in the Shinto tradition.

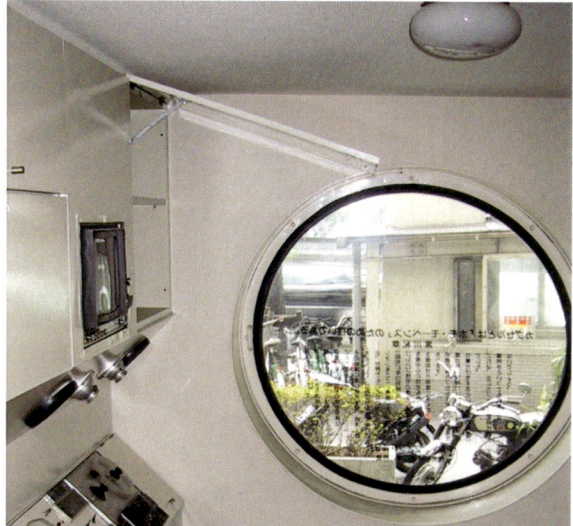

Left to right: (5) Kisho Kurokawa, Nakagin Capule Tower; (6) Capsule interior

1   Rem Koolhaas and Hans Ulrich Obrist, *Project Japan: Metabolism Talks*. Berlin: Taschen, 2011.
2   Marco Pompili, "The Structural Core as Totem," *Fabrications* 21, no. 1 (2012): 69-88.
3   Discussion of tabula rasa: symbolic clearing of land either because of a natural disaster (1929 Grand Kanto Earthquake) or war devastation (1945 American bomb attacks on Hiroshima and Nagasaki) which opens the possibilities of nothing restricting design and construction process. In Koolhaas and Obrist, *Project Japan*.
4   Günter Nitschke, *From Shinto to Ando. Studies in Architectural Anthropology in Japan*. London: Academy Press, 1993.
5   "Reinventing the City: An Interview with Architect Rem Koolhaas," *Christian Science Monitor* (20 July 2012).
6   "Permanence in Impermanence," *Japan Times* (3 October 1929).
7   Kenzo Tange and Noboru Kawazoe, *Ise: Prototype of Japanese Architecture*, Cambridge, MA: MIT Press, 1965, 206.
8   Kawazoe Noboru and Kurokawa Noriaki in Koolhaas and Obrist, *Project Japan*.
9   Nitschke, *From Shinto to Ando*.
10 Pompili, "The Structural Core as Totem," 70.
11 Discussion of myriad origins of the capsule: Kago Mobile chairs (Kurokawa), tea hut (Ekuan), Kurokawa's study of prefabricated housing in the late 1950s, a modern obsession with mobility in the form of jets and cars, the severe pressure on urban space (in 1967, the average family of 4 lives in only 2.9 rooms). In Koolhaas and Obrist, *Project Japan*.
12 Pompili, "The Structural Core as Totem."
13 Kiyonori Kikutake, "To-keishiki no kommuniti" [The Tower Shaped Community], *Kokusai Kenchiku* 25: 1 (1959): 12–19. Cited in Pompili, "The Structural Core as Totem," 74.
14   Caroline van Eck, *Organicism in Nineteenth-century Architecture: an Inquiry into Its Theoretical and Philosophical Background*. Amsterdam: Architectura et Natura Press, 1994, 168-169.
15 van Eck, *Organicism*, 170.
16 Discussion of Goethe's modified hypothesis in van Eck, *Organicism*, 107.
17 Kisho Kurokawa and eds. Peter Cachola Schmal, Ingeborg Flagge, Jochen Visscher, *Kisho Kurokawa: Metabolism and Symbiosis = Metabolismus Und Symbiosis*. (Deutsches Architekturmuseum) Berlin: Jovis, 2005.
18 Kurokawa, *Kisho Kurokawa*, 46.
19 Quote from Gottfried Semper in van Eck, *Organicism*, 228.

THE WORK OF PHILIP BEESLEY AND THE LIVING ARCHITECTURE SYSTEMS GROUP
Sarah Bonnemaison

The modern alchemist

The theme of "growth from within" resurfaces beautifully in the contemporary living architectures of Philip Beesley and the Living Architecture Systems Group [PB/LASG]. In this work, the basic units of laser-cut mylar "fronds," skeletal scaffolds, and liquid-filled glass "protocells" are like seeds sown into the design, which appear to replicate and grow as the installation occupies and infiltrates its gallery context. With each iteration of Beesley's extended research and creation program, the architecture of the frond changes, adapting to new demands, integrating robotics and sensors, all clinging onto an intricate supporting scaffold, which changes as well — as do the chemical and biological contents of the protocells. These glass bulbs filled with mysterious fluids remind us that we are entering the world of the modern alchemist. Beesley describes them as "simple models of living cells made from inorganic ingredients that exhibit some of the same properties as living cells and perform

Left to right: (1) Charron; (2) "Hylozoic" Series: "Vesica," City Gallery, Wellington, New Zealand, 2012

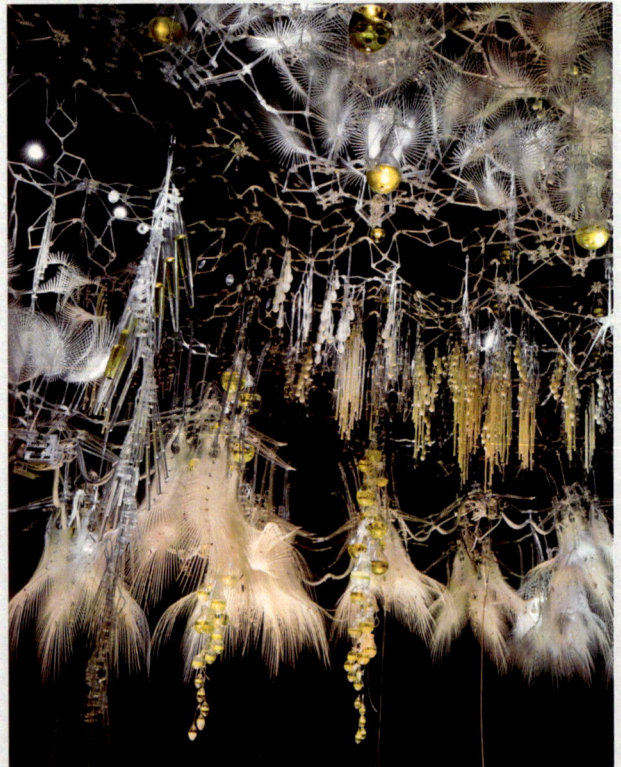

similar functions such as metabolism, movement, replication, information, evolution and self assembly."[1]

The design of the protocells may be inspired from living cells, but they are not living. And that is where the art of representing and imitating living systems comes into play. In fact, organicsm originates in the rhetoric of mimesis. The artist studies a particular natural phenomenon, imitates it, and renders a depiction of it with entirely different materials. To simply take a piece of nature and call it art would not get at the mystery and the beauty of living nature. In the organicist tradition, artifice is carefully planned to convince us of the beauty of living nature. In PB/LASG's work, the crystals of copper slowly growing in the protocells suggest to us, at a subliminal level, that they are indeed proto-cells of a living being. We cannot help but suspend our disbelief and jump into a world pregnant with future possibilities.

(3) "Sentient Chamber," National Academy of Sciences, Washington DC, 2015

From pores to spores

From one sculpture to another, the fronds and protocells combine and recombine to create an ever-more layered "skin," or web. Stepping into one of Beesley's sculptures is to step on the other side of Alice's mirror. We shrink in size, becoming like a school of fish swimming through a kelp forest. We are immersed in a skin that might be a predecessor of future building enclosures. The designer of synthetic biology suspended in glass vessels, Beesley has a plan — he wants the living systems to move ex-vitro and expand into a soft architectural skin. This plan is what gives rhetorical power to the work; the complexity and delicacy of the work is what gives beauty to the plan. In other words, we are not witnessing a game of natural geometries for its own sake, we are immersed in a thoroughly planned and carefully crafted environment that takes us from the small flask to the large immersive sculpture of fronds, and from one set of bulbous geometries to another set of radiating geometries.

From pores to spores, our eyes move from the micro to the macro. Now imagine these ideas transformed from architecture to clothing. For several years now, Beesley has been collaborating with fashion designer Iris van Herpen who, for her haute-couture collections,

(4) *Transforming Fashion, Transforming Space* exhibition: "Aegis" and the "Dome" dress, 2018.

also draws from natural phenomena: "'Aeriform' examines the nature and anatomy of air and the idea of airborne materiality and lightness, [and] 'Ludi Naturae' examines the natural and manmade landscapes of our world from a bird's-eye view, tracing the laws of entropy."[2]

In a paired exhibition, "Transforming Fashion, Transforming Space," held in 2018 at the Royal Ontario Museum, van Herpen's "Dome" dress was presented under PB/LASG's "Aegis" [Shield] sculpture. The dress is like a cloud around the body, rising towards the sculpture, which hovers over the mannequin. Made of rose-like domes, the dress is inspired from the moment when pearls of morning dew cling to the delicate skin of an insect. Watching the fashion model on the runway, "the dome dress mimics bubbles of air reflecting light and billowing around the body, producing an airy weightless movement."[3] References to nature abound here: one of the designers in the Living Architecture Systems studio shows me the inspiration — a photograph of a cricket covered with dew drops. The pearls of moisture catch the sunlight and refract color, but they will not last and the sun will soon evaporate them. Yet in that moment, the cricket enjoys his morning shower. The dome dress catches that moment.

Left to right: (5) Iris van Herpen and Philip Beesley "Dome Dress" at Aeriform runway, 2017; (6) Basalt formation, Isle of Staffa, Inner Hebrides; (7) Geometry of mannequin's skin, drawing.

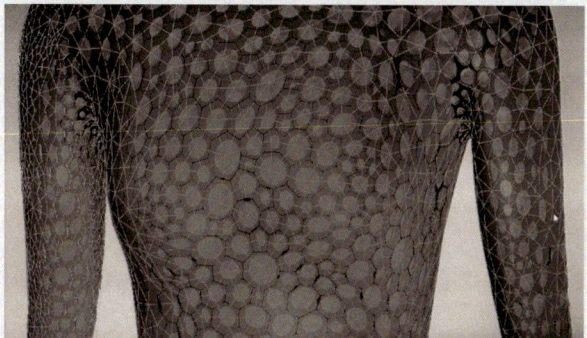

Geometries

The geometry of the mannequin's skin in the "Aegis" installation comes from the pattern visible on water's surface as it comes to a boil. The regularity of this pattern has long caught the eye of both artists and scientists. The non-linear physics of Rayleigh-Bénard determines how a liquid heated from below generates a regular pattern of convection cells: forces push the liquid up into vertical formations. For example, the hexagonal basalt rock formations on the Hebridean island of Mull are the result of these forces, formed as the volcanic lava cooled (Figure 6). PB/LASG drew from this physical phenomenon to design a stiff double-curved mesh for the mannequin (Figure 7).[4] The mesh is not merely representing this natural phenomenon, it draws on a deeper understanding of the way sliding vertical forces can inform the design of a mesh — this geometry, inspired by convection cells, is well-adapted to serve as an open web scaffold for a curved surface.

The scaffold for each installation must be sufficiently strong to support the weight of innumerable fronds and protocells, along with the electronics, power and communication networks. Yet to mimic the aesthetics and behavior of a living system, it must also be light in weight and visually transparent. Each generation of scaffold must adapt to a new space

(8) "Astrocyte," Design Exchange EDIT: Expo for Design, Innovation & Technology, Toronto, 2017

and a new design. The materials of these supporting systems allow forces to flow efficiently, and the tectonics of the joints allow the designer to interpret nature in many different ways. Not surprisingly, the geometries are derived from organic chemistry — the scaffolds can be understood as chains of hexagons and polygons branching out according to a unifying plan.

PB/LASG's most recent scaffolds are spherical. Like a sea urchin, each sphere supports fronds and spiroidal tapers radiating outwards. In order to transform a reticulated surface into a sphere, the polygons employ rectangular segments to allow the surface to curve at regular intervals. This fascination for regular geometries in nature finds its expression in this open web, much like a "Bucky Ball," inviting us to touch and wonder.

---

1   Philip Beesley, *Sibyl: Projects 2010-2012*, Kitchener, ON: Riverside Architectural Press, 70.
2   Van Herpen descriptions of the couture collection. Website accessed on 19 January 2019. https://www. irisvanherpen.com/haute-couture
3   ROM website on the exhibition.
4   Interview with Jonathan Gotfryd about the application of non-linear physics to structural design (January 17, 2019).

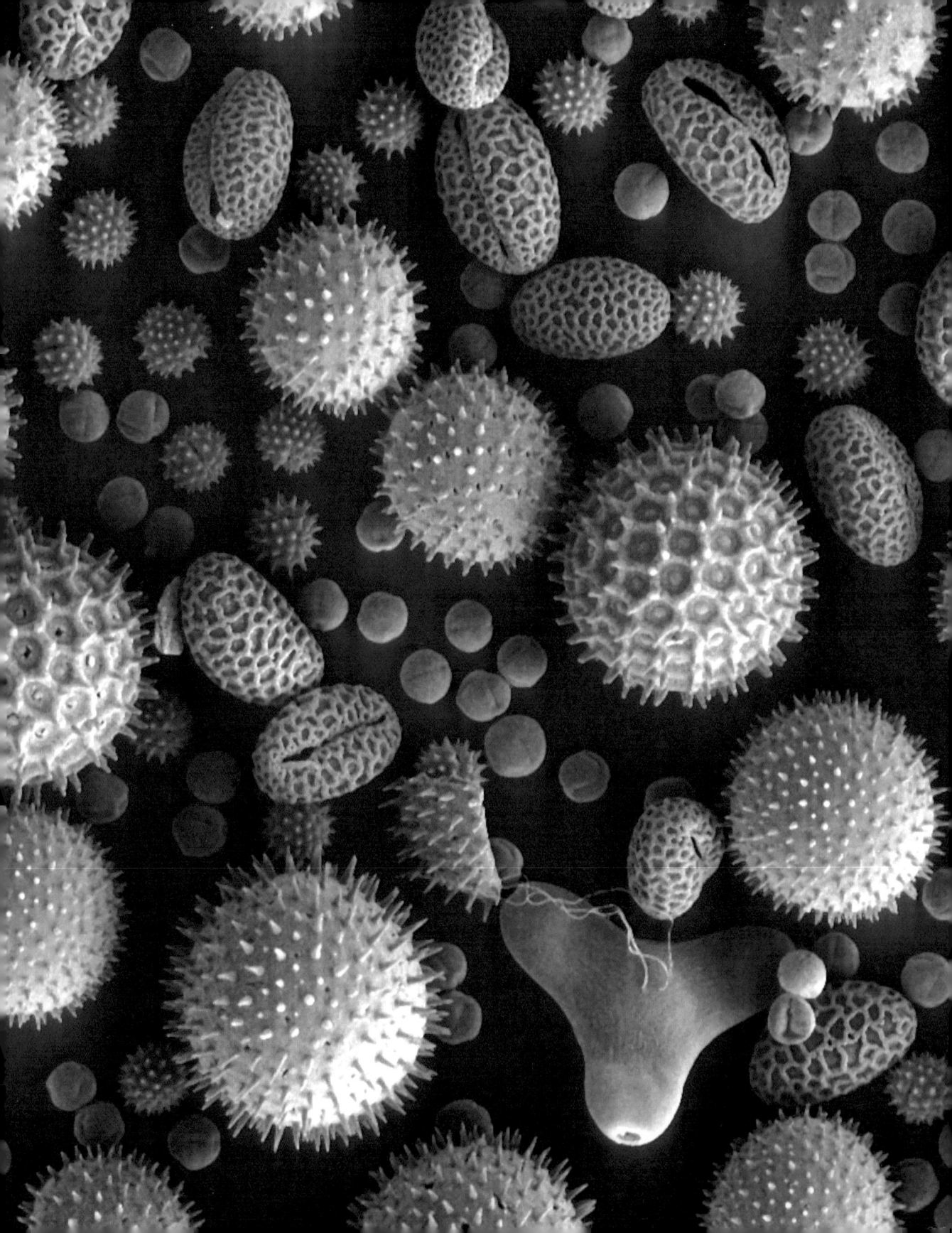

II. HARMONIC UNITY

"Originally, *concinnitas* is a rhetorical term that characterizes a style that is 'closely knit,' 'elegantly joined' or 'skillfully put together,' and therefore beautiful or elegant." This quotation by Caroline van Eck suggests that compositional harmony is an important aspect of organic beauty in architecture. Through Leon Battista Alberti's definition of *concinnitas*, this theme acknowledges the harmonic unity of the whole, which is larger than the sum of its parts.

Gottfried Semper meditated on the organicist qualities of the classical Greek column, seeing in it the flow of forces expressed in the stone capitals as they bulge out to welcome the weight of the roof. For him, the marble column expresses something that cannot be seen: the flow of forces. Similarly, Marc-Antoine Laugier's "primitive hut" is an argument for the way that architecture, as a discipline, is larger than the sum of its parts. In other words, the essential quality of the hut is more than the fact of a simple shelter made of bits and pieces — it is a metaphor for the origin of architecture itself.

Benjamin Woodward's Oxford Museum is much more than a repository for specimens of natural history; it represents a new science of construction in relation to the natural world. For John Ruskin, whose writings influenced Woodward's work, nature is the art of God. Today, the electron microscope reveals the harmonic unity that links the forms of pollen grains, diatoms, other single-celled organisms, molecules, and atoms. Architects, like scientists, are drawn to these forms and strive to mimic their beauty and complexity. And within the work of Eileen Gray and Alvar Aalto, organicism finds its modern expression as furniture, inhabitants, and a new spirituality deeply linked to nature all come into one.

The theme concludes with the material research of Brian Lilley, who explores, in the tradition of the alchemists, the physical properties of earth granules to create ceramic wall tiles with unusual properties that express the large flows of energy constantly sweeping around the Earth.

Opposite: Pollen from common plants
(sunflower, morning glory, hollyhock, lily, primrose and castor bean)

CONCINNITAS:
LEON BATTISTA ALBERTI ON ORGANIC UNITY
Ruth Vandergeest

Leon Battista Alberti (1404-74) was an Italian humanist author, artist, architect, poet, priest, linguist, philosopher, and cryptographer; he can be characterized as a Renaissance Man.[1] Alberti's reputation today is tied to his contributions to architectural theory through his work *De re aedificatoria* (On the Art of Building). In volume IX, he explores the relationship between architecture and nature, laying the foundations of organicism.[2] Alberti uses the term *concinnitas* to define architectural beauty:

> Architecture consists of two parts, the *lineamenta* and the *materia*: the former derive from the mind, the latter from nature. Thus, as a constituent of *concinnitas*, *finitio* may be understood as the unification of lineamenta and materia by the architect.[3]

Architectural theorists have attempted to define *concinnitas*, but with little agreement. To explore the various definitions and implications it is important to know Alberti's explanation in *De re aedificatoria*; various writers have emphasized different parts of the excerpt above to various ends. Leo Leoni and Walther Flemming defined concinnitas quite literally, using ideas of number, finishing, and collocation, and quantity, quality, and relation in their respective works.[4] Joan Gadol also considers Alberti's mathematical definition of beauty via proportions, connecting Alberti's concinnitas to Vitruvius through the Vitruvian theory of *symmetria*.[5] Caroline van Eck emphasizes the importance of knowing the rhetorical background and the practical craftsmanship; she characterizes concinnitas as "'closely knit', 'elegantly joined' or 'skillfully put together', and therefore beautiful or elegant."[6]

Van Eck draws attention to aspects of planning and the foresight that Leoni and Flemming did not consider:

> Socrates and Aristotle, in the 4th century BC, speak to the relationship of the body's unity without considering mathematical proportion. Plato quoted Socrates' teachings about the importance of unity, comparing the structure of a speech to the composition of a living being. Socrates argued that all parts of the body with their unique purposes contribute to the proper functioning of a body. Whereas Aristotle also compares the

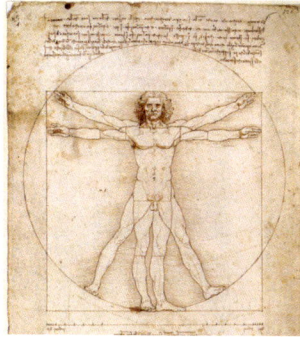

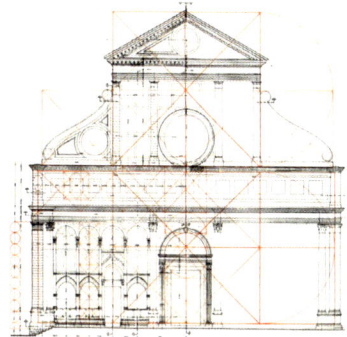

Left to right: (1) Leon Battista Alberti, presumed self-portrait in bronze, c.1435; (2) Vitruvian Man by Leonardo da Vinci, ca. 1492; (3) Proportional study of Alberti's Santa Maria Novella

necessity of poetic structure to accomplish unity, via the metaphor of a whole creature.[7]

Vitruvius furthers the idea of the body as a symbol of unity in *On the Art of Building*, noting the necessity of proportion. He used the proportions of an ideal human body as a method to create unity: the circle and square, perfect shapes representative of infinite God and man, respectively, could express the idea of *homo quadratus*, the ideal human body circumscribed on the circle and square (Figure 2).[8] The circumscribed man served as a connection to the Divine. In Genesis 1:26, God says, "Let us make mankind in our image, in our likeness."[9] Divine shapes, the circle and square, overlaid on divine expression of an ideal human body, informed Vitruvius' views on what ideal proportions are.

It is important to note that Alberti did not necessarily associate mathematical proportions with beauty. Concinnitas, as he defines it, also includes the reconciliation of opposites, which Alberti compared to polyphonic music of the Renaissance, writing "Variety is always a most pleasing spice."[10] Theorists like the ones mentioned previously have said that the chief characteristic of concinnitas is proportion of the module throughout a building, though even Alberti did not adhere to that concept. Proportional studies of Alberti's work often reveal the use of multiple proportional modules (Figure 3).[11] To Alberti, modular proportion can serve the overall unity of a structure, but overall unity can also be attained by the organization of qualitative oppositions. Concinnitas, then, unifies opposition and variety.[12] The harmonious whole, an aspect of concinnitas, would be ruined if even one module were not included, because the various proportions are rationally organized in such a way that every single one is a necessary part of the whole.[13]

An example, which demonstrates Caroline van Eck's idea of foresight and planning of concinnitas, is Cologne Cathedral. The cathedral has undergone many renovations and alterations since its foundation stone was laid in 1248.[14] The most recent upgrade to the building, occurring in 2007, was the replacement of 19th century windows destroyed during the Second World War.[15] Through various stages of construction and events in history, the cathedral continues to stand as an example of organic unity that has persisted through centuries.

Construction of what is called the "old cathedral" began around 800 AD, over the location of the previous church. It was consecrated in 873 and remained unchanged until construction of the "new cathedral" began in 1248.[16] The impetus for the cathedral's expansion was the Pope's gift to the archbishop, in 1164, of relics of the three Magi, or wise men, from the story of Christ's birth. These are among the most important relics of the Catholic faith; their prominence led the cathedral to become one of the most significant pilgrimage sites in Europe.

The cathedral that is known today (Figure 4) was built in phases that reflected the progressive destruction of the older building. As each portion was demolished, a new section was built as a replacement and consecrated, the cycle repeating itself with successive portions of the building. This incremental construction continued until 1520, when it was interrupted — leaving the cathedral's towers uncompleted and a wooden crane on one of them as the landmark of Cologne — until construction resumed 300 years later, in 1823.

In 1842, the final foundation stone was laid, marking the final phase of the cathedral's construction. The architects and builders followed plans drawn over 600 years earlier (though including modern engineering) and the work was completed in 1880. By this time, the cathedral was valued as a national monument to the German people. The funding for the final stretch of construction was procured through the royal purse and the Zentral-Dombau-Verein (ZDV), an association set up by the citizens of Cologne to raise money for the completion of their cathedral; it eventually collected 60% of the funds required.

During the Second World War, the cathedral sustained serious damage (Figure 5), but remained one of the few buildings still standing in Cologne at the war's end. Before much of the bombing began, the windows and relics were removed, and Medieval art sandbagged. Reconstruction after the war continued until 1956, at which time the cathedral workshop turned to conservation of the building.

The Cologne Cathedral exemplifies concinnitas because it represents organic unity through many parts and particularly because of the foresight required for its completion. Through the centuries the cathedral has had many renovations and changes, deepening its value to Cologne and as an architectural destination. If one part of it were not completed as it was, the cathedral would not be the successful or beautiful whole encapsulated by the idea of concinnitas.

Left to right: (4) Cologne Cathedral; (5) Aerial view of the cathedral in 1944

1   Caroline van Eck, *Goethe and Alberti: Organic Unity in Nature and Architecture*. Saskatoon: University of Saskatchewan, 1995), 24.
2   van Eck, *Goethe and Alberti*, 23.
3   Robert William Tavenor, *Concinnitas in the Architectural Theory and Practice of Leon Battista Alberti*. Cambridge: University of Cambridge, 1985, 5.
4   Tavenor, *Concinnitas*, 3.
5   Tavenor, *Concinnitas*, 1.
6   van Eck, *Goethe and Alberti*, 41.
7   Caroline van Eck, *Organicism in Nineteenth Century Architecture: an Inquiry Into its Theoretical and Philosophical Background*. Amsterdam: Architectura et Natura Press, 1994, 41-42.
8   van Eck, *Organicism*, 42.
9   Genesis 1:26 (NIV)
10 van Eck, *Organicism*, 53.
11 Tavenor, *Concinnitas*, 3.
12 van Eck, *Organicism*, 40.
13 Tavenor, *Concinnitas*, 3.
14 Matthias Deml, "A Brief History of Cologne Cathedral". Website Kölner Dom [Cologne Cathedral]. https://www.koelner-dom.de/geschichte/a-brief-history-of-cologne-cathedral/?L=1
15 Robert Lewis, "Cologne Cathedral." *Encyclopedia Britannica*. (2019 / October 17, 2018); https://www.britannica.com/topic/Cologne-Cathedral

THE VILLA MAIREA: CONCEPTS OF THE WHOLE
John Follet

The Villa Mairea, in Noormarku, Finland (Figure 1), was built during a period in architecture when functional design and modular reproduction were ascendant, and the "International" style of architecture was being promoted in museums and professional journals. It is named after its client, heiress and arts patron Maire Gullichsen (née Ahlström) who, with her husband Harry Gullichsen, was a friend and kindred spirit to Alvar and Aino Aalto. Maire Gullichsen had partnered with the Aaltos to form Artek, which fabricated the Aaltos' furniture. The Aaltos felt that functionalism alone lacked many of the attributes that provide a building with a source of meaning, inspiration and emotional rootedness, and the Gullichsens shared this view.[1] In his design for the Villa Mairea, Alvar Aalto did not entirely reject the stringency of functionalism, but used it as one of various components within the design.

The Villa Mairea is composed of a robust and constantly changing array of materials that speak to their surroundings: it is part of the forest and seeks to express its beauty. Critics have described the villa as a type of synthesis

> between nature and culture, between something natural and something man made, something that evolves and something that is composed, something that connotes the past and something that looks to the future.[2]

This statement speaks to the type of unity which Aalto intended for the design, bringing together opposing elements as he proposed a new way of thinking about the modern home. In many ways it exhibits *concinnitas*, referring to Alberti's definition of "that unity, given by nature to her creations, which is based on purposive unity of carrying and opposing elements."[3] Through the Villa Mairea's many attributes and inspirations, Aalto achieves a type of harmony between user and landscape, be it natural or synthetic.

Alberti tells us that we should, "like the Ancients, imitate nature," which he calls the "supreme artist or maker."[4] However, it was Aalto's inclusion of nature, and abstracted elements, that in his early career brought him much unwanted attention:

Above: (1) Atelier tower and garden, Villa Mairea; Below: (2) Living room stair; (3) Conservatory

he "was held in suspicion by many Finnish architects for an emerging indigenous architecture of the type previously condemned in Saarinen, [and] Sonck."[5] While Le Corbusier employed mathematically-placed concrete columns in a "free plan," Aalto by contrast evoked an internal forest within the Villa Mairea by positioning tree trunks seemingly at random (Figure 2). His affinity for Japanese concepts of nature is exemplified in his use of "shoji" style windows (Figure 3), in which the slender wood mullions that divide each pane of glass create an effect as if one were looking through a wall of bamboo. The ubiquitous presence of natural light, juxtaposed to the internal forest, create the illusion that one is neither fully indoors nor outdoors (Figure 4). The villa's composition of a wide range of materials — including steel,

Left to right: (4) Maire and Aino at the Villa Mairea, 1940s; (5) Sauna door

concrete, stone, brick and, most prominently, wood — has led critics such as Sarah Menin to suggest that "the volatile alliance between differences is stabilized by conceptualizing it in terms of oppositional pairs, such as thick and thin, simple/complex and others."[6] Alberti believed unity could be achieved through the varying of "aspects of ... forms according to their purpose, by making them more or less strong or frail.[7]

For Aalto, the unity of the villa would be achieved through the integration of functionalism with nature, which further required a type of contextual consideration that spoke to Finnish culture. While many modernist architects sought newness for its own sake, for Aalto, tradition did "not imply regressive traditionalism, but ... [as] a source of meaning, inspiration and emotional rooting."[8] One example of this is the front door to the outdoor sauna located at the rear of the property (Figure 5). At first glance, the door appears to be comprised of a random and overlapping assortment of wood, but on closer examination, it resembles a type of quilt found in many Finnish homes. Aalto understood that while architectural types and styles change, by instituting elements of culture and tradition, buildings can continue to hold relevance beyond their time. He took much of his aesthetic inspiration from traditional Finnish vernacular, most specifically the 19th century Niemelä Farmstead (Figure 6), which exemplifies the use of wood and a union with nature.

Through his design of the Villa Mairea, "Aalto finally freed himself... from formal functionalism and achieved the organic."[9] Through the appropriate and well-considered use of what has been termed oppositional pairs, he created a harmonious unity. Extrapolating from Aristotelian discourse, van Eck writes that "the unity of opposing and varying qualities referred to as *concinnitas* is made possible because the maker acts according to a logically prior plan or concept of the whole, by which all the parts and the relations between these and the whole are regulated and determined."[10] In this understanding, it can be said that Alvar Aalto achieved a type of concinnitas or oppositional unity, within the design of the Villa Mairea.

(6) Yard of the Niemelä farm, Seurasaari Open Air Museum, Helsinki

1   Sarah Menin and Flora Samuel, *Nature and Space: Aalto and Le Corbusier*. New York: Routledge, 2003, 135.
2   Menin and Samuel, *Nature and Space*, 137.
3   Caroline van Eck, *Organicism in Nineteenth Century Architecture, an enquiry into its theoretical and philosophical background*. Amsterdam: Architecture et Natura Press, 1994, 50.
4   van Eck, *Organicism*, 49.
5   Roger Connah, *Finland: Modern Architectures in History*, London: Reaktion Books, 2005, 83.
6   Menin and Samuel, *Nature and Space*, 137.
7   van Eck, *Organicism*, 49.
8   Juhani Pallasmaa, "From Tectonic to Painterly Architecture," *Encounters*, Helsinki: Rakennustieto, 2005, 215.
9   Louna Lahti, *Aalto: 1898-1976 Paradise for the Man in the Street*, Berlin: Taschen, 2004, 43.
10 van Eck, *Organicism*.

THE HEART OF SCHOOL AT GREEN SCHOOL: BAMBOO AS MATERIAL ORGANICISM
Michael MacLean

The bamboo architecture at the Heart of School, at Green School in Bali, designed by the architecture firm Ibuku, demonstrates Caroline van Eck's understanding of organicism as it threads together ideas from Leon Battista Alberti, Claude Perrault, and Marc-Antoine Laugier. This building represents something which is greater than the sum of its parts: it creates harmony through its use of a single material and central basket columns, as well as positive beauty through its micro and macro symmetry. Further, the bamboo imposes its laws on the end result, through the process of bamboo model making. Thus, by weaving together a material as simple as bamboo, the whole — that is, the building — becomes a beautifully crafted and functional organic structure.

Van Eck describes Alberti's concept of *concinnitas* as a "regulating factor... by which unity and therefore beauty are achieved."[1] The Heart of School exemplifies this concept in its central basket columns and nearly exclusive use of bamboo. The careful craftsmanship and engineering of this building — using a traditional and low-cost material — creates a visual continuity and apparently seamless joinery that speaks to our contemporary understanding of Alberti's concinnitas: "a style that is 'closely knit', 'elegantly joined' or 'skilfully put together', and therefore beautiful or elegant."[2]

The central basket columns seen in the plan can be seen as the "bones" of the structure in the same way that bones form the structure of our bodies (Figure 1a). Without the central basket columns, the Heart of School cannot stand.[3] Their woven structure gives this light material the ability to support the structural elements of the building: its roof, beams and 2,740 sq m of floor over three levels (Figure 1b).

All movement in the building spirals around the three central basket columns, either beginning or ending at them. Ibuku's use of bamboo pin joinery contributes to the building's near mono-materiality, thus aligning it with Alberti's concinnitas: the single material generates a continuity in texture, colour and visual language that creates an organic beauty and unity.

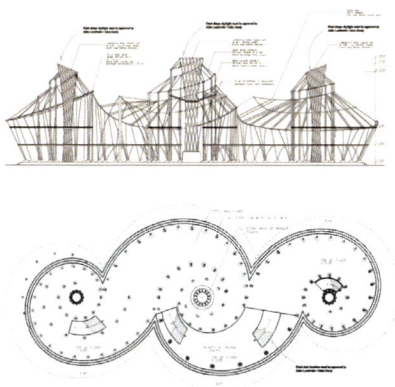

Left to right: (1a) Plan and (1b) Section; (2) Heart of School, Green School, Bali

The Heart of School at Green School exemplifies Perrault's definition of symmetry and positive beauty through its global and material symmetry, as seen in the building's plan, elevation and construction details. The physical flexibility and versatility of bamboo as a material enables bamboo architecture to achieve organic symmetry as Perrault defines it:

> Consider symetrie, and not proportion, as positive beauty, founded on convincing reasons: the fact that relations between parts and the whole could be easily perceived, based as they are on equality and similarity in the positioning, dimensions, and ordering of the parts.[4]

As previously discussed, the building is composed of three circular volumes spiraling out from the central basket columns. These columns create symmetry in two ways: in elevation, where the middle column creates a vertical mirror line; and in plan, where a line of symmetry can be drawn through all three columns. In addition to this larger symmetry in section and plan, the bamboo itself reveals a micro symmetry in its internal structure (Figure 4). The building's interior barriers and screens, as well as its handrails, use milled bamboo to reveal these cross sections. Thus, through plan, section, and material, this building demonstrates organic symmetry, contributing to its positive beauty.

The architectural essence and grounding of Ibuku's buildings, and particularly this school building, conform with Marc-Antoine Laugier's understanding of organicism, with its emphasis on material and tectonic aspects.[5] The way bamboo grows informs the way it is used, exemplifying van Eck's conception of tectonic organicism, in which nature is a model for constructional procedure.[6] Likewise, in his search for the essence of architecture and beauty, Laugier radically separates ornament and structure and returns to the essential principles of architecture: "the principles are based on nature herself ('*la simple nature*'): her methods and procedures are the foundation for the rules of architecture."[7] Laugier explains that architecture must not follow the appearance of nature, but rather its laws.[8] It is in this fundamental understanding of following the laws of nature that the Heart of

Left to right: (3) Construction

School demonstrates tectonic organicism through its design process. Ibuku uses scaled bamboo models as a primary tool for design.[9] The use of scale models to design bamboo structures is an efficient way of harnessing the material's "embodied information"[10] towards the design process, since bamboo behaves in a scale model very similalry to the way it does at full scale. Thus, the nature of bamboo as a material informs the tectonics of how one builds with it, which in turn influences the form of the building — resulting in a beauty directed by the laws of nature.

Laugier's tectonics, Perrault's symmetry, and Alberti's harmony all describe the organic beauty of the Heart of School at Green School, making it an excellent example of architecture in which the whole is larger than the sum of its parts. While both traditional and contemporary examples of bamboo architecture provide material for inspiration, Ibuku's Heart of School at Green School in Bali is a superlative contemporary example of bamboo in organicist architecture.

1   Caroline van Eck, *Organicism in Nineteenth-century Architecture: an Inquiry into Its Theoretical and Philosophical Background*. Amsterdam: Architectura et Natura Press, 1994, 49.
2   van Eck, *Organicism*, 45.
3   Bamboo U. "Bamboo U Faculty." bamboou.com. https://bamboou.com/about/ (accessed October 14). Hardy and Ibuku credit engineer Jorg Stamm with developing the basket column concept.
4   van Eck, *Organicism*, 87.
5   van Eck, *Organicism*, 6.
6   van Eck, *Organicism*, 25.
7   Marc-Antoine Laugier, *Essai sur l'Architecture*, 1755, 8.
8   Laugier, (Note 66), xlv.
9   Elora Hardy. "Magical Houses, Made of bamboo". Lecture, Ted 2015. Vancouver, Canada. March 2015. https://.wwww.ted.com/talks/elora_hardy_magical_houses_made_of_bamboo?quote=703
10 Emmanuel Jannasch. "Embodied Information in Structural Timber," in *Structures and Architecture: New Concepts, Applications, and Challenges*, ed. Paulo Cruz, London: CRC Press, 2013, 2176–83.

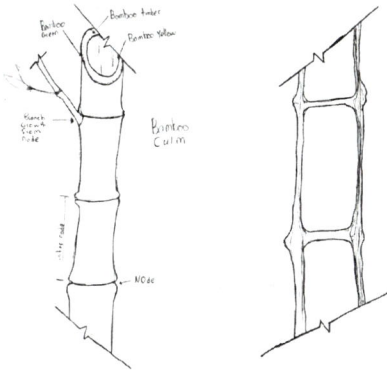

(4) Cross-section through bamboo

(5) Interior, showing the bamboo basket columns

YASMEEN LARI'S CHULAH STOVES, PAKISTAN
Jaudat Adnan

Yasmeen Lari (1941-), one of Pakistan's best-known architects and the designer of many landmark buildings in Karachi, is best known internationally for her work in rural development and efforts to improve the life of rural women. In this work, she is inspired by the words of Egyptian architect Hassan Fathy,

> You must start from the beginning, letting your new buildings grow from the daily lives of the people who will live in them, shaping the houses to the measure of people's songs, weaving the pattern of a village as if on the village looms, mindful of the trees and the crafts that grow there, respectful of the skylines and humble before the seasons.[1]

In 1980, Lari co-founded the Heritage Foundation of Pakistan with her husband, historian Suhail Zaheer Lari, for heritage conservation research and advocacy. Following the earthquake of 2005, she began promoting women-centred sustainable building techniques using bamboo, lime, and mud, realizing more than 45,000 green (zero carbon) shelters for disaster relief. Her aim is to make buildings that not only have small carbon footprints, but are also simple enough to be built by those in need.

Yasmeen Lari's Pakistan Chulah project exemplifies this understanding. A *chulah* (also called *chulha*) is a modest earthen stove commonly used in Pakistan and India. Built directly on the ground, it presents many problems:

> Kareema is a beggar woman who lives with her family of mendicants in the shadow of the World Heritage necropolis Makli, Thatta. All her life she has used a 3-brick floor mounted smoke-emitting stove, mixing dust and ground pollution with the food that she cooks. Come rain or floods, the stove gets washed away, leaving her with no possibility of cooked food for her family even if some philanthropists provide bags of rice or flour.[2]

Lari turned her attention to the problem of this traditional stove. First, she improved the design by expanding the stove to include double combustion chambers, an air intake pipe, a chimney to reduce smoke exposure for the women using it, utensil

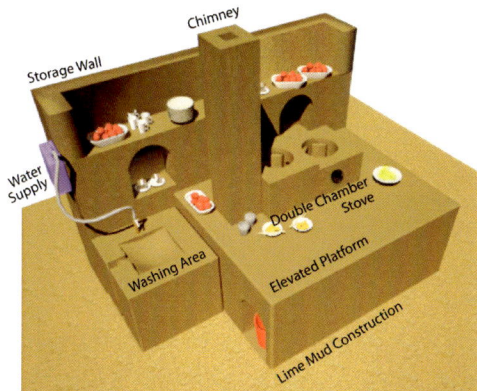

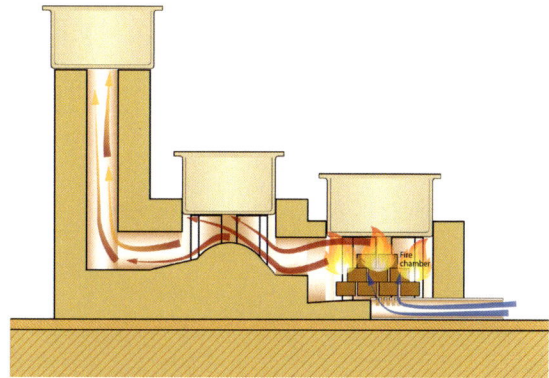

Left to right: (1) Axonometric view of the chulah; (2) Cross section, showing the heating element and chimney

storage, and a washing area. To ensure the stove would withstand flooding, she raised it on a platform and added powdered limestone to the earthen mix.

Although Lari does not identify herself as an organic architect, the methods she employs manifest the ideologies of organicism. According to Frank Lloyd Wright,

> organic can merely mean something biological but if you are going to take the word organic into your consciousness as concerned entities, something in which the part is to the whole as the whole is to the part, and which is all devoted to a purpose consistently, then you have something that can live because that is vital.[3]

Caroline van Eck describes Goethe's approach to organicism as "concepts developed with the aim to understanding the laws of growth and form in living nature."[4] Lari's work echoes this, not through the architecture's formal qualities but by planting a seed — the stove — and letting the seed grow into a tree.

By raising the stove's earthen platform above the ground, which is frequently a dirty environment, the Pakistan Chulah improves hygiene for the whole family. It has become a life-transforming avenue for the women who use it, literally raising their status — previously, they had to crouch on the floor in a posture of helplessness; the raised platform, by contrast, creates a space that allows women to sit in an erect posture and gives them a dining and gathering space. For the first time, the stove provides its users with a space that can be used for socializing with family members and the community.

To promote uptake of the improved design, and to provide a means through which rural women could afford to build such a stove, the Heritage Foundation of Pakistan began to train "stove sisters" — these are rural master trainers, mostly non-literate, who visit nearby villages and train housewives to build the stove.[5] They also provide hygiene training to encourage hand-washing prior to cooking and handling food. Each stove sister charges US$2, which amounts to 200 rupees, to provide guidance in mixing lime and mud, as well as guidelines for the stove construction. The family incurs $8 in total costs, including the fee paid to the stove sister. Although this is a

Left to right: (3) Personalization of the chulah; (4) A community hub

considerable amount — it may equal up to half a month's income for some — the long-term benefits of the stove prove its value. One stove sister helped build 20,000 stoves, earning a direct profit of US$40,000; this shows the success of the Heritage Foundation's strategy. The economic benefits to women who teach other women how to make the stoves is part of this process, in which something small grows into something larger.

Lastly, the stove's platform provides a space that can be modified and changed according to the needs of its user; for example, some women with stoves have started making glazed tiles, clay products, and textiles. The stove not only provides these women a space for such work, but a platform for selling it. Although each stove is fundamentally the same, as its owner decorates her stove, she personalizes it and adds ornamentation inherited over generations. Frank Lloyd Wright explains,"the matter of ornament is primarily a spiritual one, a proof of culture, an expression of the quality of the soul within us, easily enjoyed by the enlightened when it is a real expression of ourselves."[6] This spiritual and cultural sense is evident in the Chulah stoves: their decorations are a proof of a cultural expression and play an important role in belonging to the community.

Lari's Chulah stoves provide women with an accessible way to better their everyday lives. In this, they are similar to Alejandro Aravena's "half a good house" concept for a social housing project in Chile, which provides poor families with a structure divided in two: a dwelling for themselves in one half, and a void in the other to fill according to their needs and finances.[7] Both projects support the creativity of the owners and the possibilities for development over time. Van Eck states that

> Goethe believed that all the parts of a plant were variations and developments from one seminal element. This was the primordial leaf, which might appear as a leaf, a flower or a seed capsule. All advanced parts of a plant could be regarded as transformations of one single, basic organ.[8]

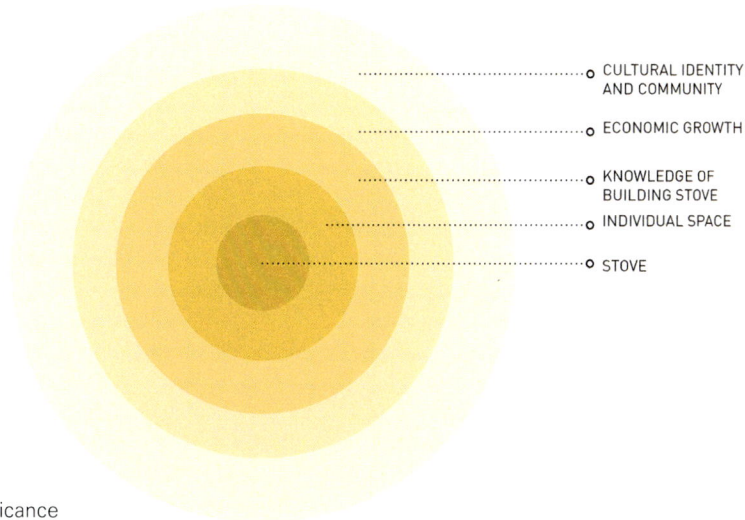

CULTURAL IDENTITY
AND COMMUNITY

ECONOMIC GROWTH

KNOWLEDGE OF
BUILDING STOVE

INDIVIDUAL SPACE

STOVE

(5) Nested significance

Both Lari and Aravena follow the concept of self-build and self-help by planting a seed in the community and letting it grow over time, taking its natural, unique course.

Yasmeen Lari's work has not only contributed to rural communities; it has a ripple effect. In communities where the stove has been implemented, the Heritage Foundation has been able to implement multiple programs to improve village life, including better-constructed shelters, eco-toilets, raised earthen platform water pumps, community women's centres, and community forests.[9] The theory that "the whole is larger then the sum of its parts" is clearly evident in Yasmeen Lari's work. Its value can be seen in all the communities her work has touched, as design improves the quality and dignity of their lives.

1   Brinda Somaya and Urvashi Mehta. *An Emancipated Place* (The Proceedings of the conference and exhibition Women in Architecture, and a conference on the work of women architects, focus South Asia, February, 2000). Mumbai: Hecar Foundation, 2000.
2   Yasmeen Lari, "Pakistan Chulah," *Domus Magazine* (13 January 2017). https://www.domusweb.it/en/architecture/2017/01/03/the_pakistan_chulah.html
3   Frank Lloyd Wright, *Truth against the World: Frank Lloyd Wright Speaks for an Organic Architecture*. New York: Wiley, 1992, 51.
4   Caroline van Eck, *Organicism in Nineteenth-century Architecture: An Inquiry into Its Theoretical and Philosophical Background*. Amsterdam: Architectura et Natura Press, 1994, 101.
5   All from Lari, "Pakistan Chulah."
6   Frank Lloyd Wright, *Truth against the World*, 71.
7   "Half A House Builds A Whole Community: Elemental's Controversial Social Housing," *ArchDaily* (October 18, 2016).
8   Sarah Bonnemaison, "What is Organicism?" Lecture Notes, September 2018.
9   Yasmeen Lari, "The First Comprehensive Report on Green Shelters," Heritage Foundation of Pakistan (2018). https://s3.amazonaws.com/data.hoggit.com/12738.

CERAMIC DYNAMICS
Brian Lilley

Our interdisciplinary research group bridges art and science to investigate ceramic material and production techniques and *in situ* environmental interactions as part of larger organic systems. Led by Brian Lilley, Rory Macdonald and Aaron Outhwaite, we work in the fields of architecture, art, and material science respectively. Our previous projects have explored sustainable design of gardens and walls, interior humidity absorption, and gentle microclimatic adaptations. Out of this work, porosity has been a key consideration across scales and disciplines.

Our departure point is the character of ceramics as a material. Kevin Plucknett describes ceramics as having a wide range of performance advantages when compared with other materials: they are harder and stiffer than metals or polymers, have significantly better resistance to wear and corrosion, and are generally of lower density. For these reasons, ceramics are used in a diverse variety of applications: from simple building materials through to space shuttle thermal tiles, wear-resistant coatings, and automotive turbocharger rotors. But ceramics are also brittle materials; within the microstructure of ceramics, physical interactions such as cracking occur at the scale from millimeters to microns.[1]

Current work introducing organic compounds into ceramics may produce new material attributes that minimize such degradation. Some materials researchers are turning to organic chemistry as a way of improving the performance attributes of ceramics. Aaron Outhwaite's work, for example, explores the integration of microalgae in ceramics, and their effects on material chemistry at the micro- to nanometer scale.[2] Algae in its natural state is an abundant material, gathered as seaweed from the North Atlantic shoreline. The seaweed mass yields 30-40% biopolymer and the harvesting process leaches out impurities and sea salts. The biopolymer is then mixed with local clay bodies, and tested across a range of drying, firing, and glazing techniques. Material characterization tests define possible uses and production techniques, such as the mixture best suited for 3D printing.

Additive Manufacturing (AM) has added new possibilities for the production of ceramic building systems. From the scale of a tile to the scale of a building, AM capabilities allow for parametric flexibility from unit to unit. This is useful for varying size, degree of porosity and color of the tile, as seen in the *Porosity Wall* study (2018) (Figure 1).

Microclimate reflects both local climate and environmental conditions. The two constantly interact, with "flow" — driven by solar radiation — being the central process, creating wind patterns and the hydrologic cycle. Important flow characteristics, such as potential solar gain or freeze-thaw cycles, can be mapped within a material. Local materials and vegetation are already adapted to local climates — defined, for example, by planting regions across North America. Lstiburek has suggested that the porosity of vapour barriers should also be related to climate region, which may in turn influence a wall's composition, direction, and organization.[3]

Top to bottom: (1) *Porosity Wall*, 2018 (2) Tile study for *Moss Garden*, 2016

The *Moss Garden* competition entry for the Jardin de Métis explores such considerations — wind patterns, the hydrologic cycle, and shading — in a ceramic tile assembly (Fig. 2).

Any modification of a microclimate is related to human sensibilities and physical needs.[4] Our approach is directed towards making low-impact material and system adaptations that improve human comfort. While shielding and enclosure play an important role, flow dynamics are also important to consider, when shaping design criteria for building materials. Testing materials *in situ*, over time, is critical.

A Smart Geometries workshop from 2012, *Transgranular Perspiration*, used embedded sensors to map heat dissipation and moisture migration in composite ceramic materials (Figures 3-5).[5] Workshop participants layered unfired clay onto fired tile substrates, and then used Bentley System's *GenerativeComponents* software to model "how pore dimensions, viscosity, and the depth of the porous surface affect absorption and release ... at different scales."[6] The iterative process of modelling, rapid prototyping, and measuring allowed the team to quickly evolve new tile configurations and change their surface patterns to decrease cracking and improve substrate bonding.

Biological systems are an important inspiration for design research, demonstrating how living material systems function. The tree, for example, is marvelous in its adaptive qualities to changing conditions, such as solar exposure and shade, surface transport

of water, porosity, and absorption. Similarly, human skin exhibits both active surfaces and composite layers to regulate bodily functions and find equilibrium. In the *Porosity Brick* project (2018), biomimicry was a starting point, using ceramic layers of different porosity to store moisture, creating a passive humidity "flywheel" effect, in which moisture is gradually released over time (Figure 6).

Why is the design of ceramic gradients, porosity, and directionality important to an organic architecture? Considering ceramic materials as passive environmental modulators of temperature and humidity, porosity allows for absorption, directionality allows for transportation, and a gradient allows for a dynamic combination of heat energy and moisture content. The design of the material can be seen as a combination of these functions, together with its lightweight structural capabilities. We must also consider efficient material use. If the performance of a standard material can be enhanced, then the use of the material can be differentiated and refined toward specific environmental or programmatic criteria. The composition of a ceramic wall in a bathroom, for example, should vary from that of a public lobby. Furthermore, by allowing standard materials to take on more specified roles in environmental modulation, the need for mechanical environmental regulation systems will be reduced.

To create gradients of porosity in ceramics, "fugitive" fillers can be employed that are removed at some stage of processing, leaving remnant pores that resemble the original filler material in their shape. Examples of common fillers include carbon (e.g. graphite) or biomaterials such as starches. The latter are effectively renewable resources, and contain only ~25 atomic percent

(3) Tile scaffold, *Transgranular Perspiration* workshop, 2012

carbon, which is more environmentally acceptable; starches also have the benefit of being available in a variety of sizes, depending upon the original plant source.

It is possible to vary the amount of pore-forming filler through the material, creating a functional gradient, which can be achieved using techniques such as "tape casting;" this approach involves processing fluid suspensions into thin layers that can be laminated together. Another interesting approach for producing "oriented" porosity involves freezing aqueous suspensions. When sufficiently cooled, ice crystals form in a suspension of fine particles, growing away from the cooled surface (Figure 7). The ice growth pattern depends on a variety of parameters, including the suspension characteristics (e.g. viscosity, solids loading, and particle size) and the temperature (i.e. the degree of "under-cooling" below the freezing point of the liquid). The ice is then removed by sublimation, leaving pores in the shapes of disappeared crystals.

Transferring technical ceramic processes from the micro to the macro scale is a long range investigation; however, both partial sintering and freeze-casting present viable, relatively inexpensive processes to achieve porosity and/or directionality with minimal shrinkage. Considering the next prototype, the introduction of phase change materials will significantly increase the thermal storage capacity and hence the levelling factor of the thermal mass. Vollen and Clifford's eco-ceramic facades provide an example of how ceramic vessels filled with phase-change material can be sculpted to work with specific sun angles for passive environmental benefit.[7]

Top to bottom: *Transgranular Perspiration*: (4) Visualizing heat dissipation and moisture migration with GenerativeComponents software; (5) Tile surface variations.

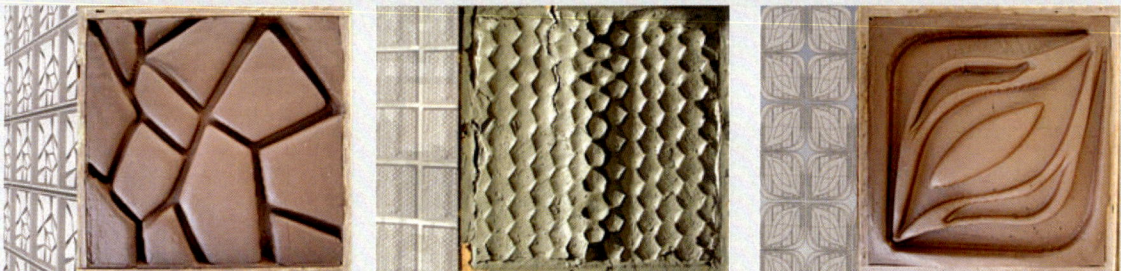

DESIGN RESEARCH FOLIO

With respect to architectural design and expression, this research is grounded in traditional and cultural building techniques such as amphorae and rammed earth building, but also includes present-day technologies such as desiccants, space shuttle tiles, and bio-ceramics. In each case, ceramic's internal microstructure engages larger environmental phenomena at the exposed surface. Given that temporal flow is an important consideration, aspects of filtering and recycling, scaffolding, and plant growth can potentially lead to a heightened awareness of an everyday phenomenology of place.

1   Michael F. Ashby, Hugh Shercliff and David Cebon. *Materials: engineering, science, processing and design*. Oxford: Butterworth-Heinemann, 2007.
2   Aaron Outhwaite, "The characterization of a building-integrated microalgae photobioreactor," (Master of Applied Sciences Thesis), Dalhousie University, 2015.
3   Joseph Lstiburek. "Vapor barriers and wall design," *Building Science Press* (November) 2004.
4   Kyle Steinfeld, Pravin Bhiwapurkar, Anna Dyson, and Jason Vollen. "Situated Bioclimatic Information Design: a new approach to the processing and visualization of climate data," *ACADIA* 2010: 88-96.
5   The *Transgranular Perspiration* Workshop Cluster at ACADIA 2012 was led by Brian Lilley, Roly Hudson and Kevin Plucknett, Dalhousie University. See also Kevin Plucknett and Brian Lilley, "The art of engineering nothing (or what we can do to 'design' porous ceramics)," *Smart Geometry 2012*.
6   Angus W. Stocking, "Transgranular perspiration is not sandy sweat: new discoveries in ceramic tiles at SmartGeometry 2012," *Informed Infrastructure*. Accessed January 22, 2019. http://informedinfrastructure.com/239/transgranular-perspiration-is-not-sandy-sweat-new-discoveries-in-ceramic-tiles-at-smartgeometry-2012/
7   Jason Vollen and Dale Clifford. "Porous boundaries: material transitions from territories to maps," in *Matter: material processes in architectural production*, eds. Gail P. Borden and Michael Meredith. New York: Routledge, 2012, 155-169.

This page, left to right: (6) Microstructure characteristics in variable porosity ceramic unit; (7) Ice crystals.
Opposite page: *Porosity Brick*: (8-10) Tile surface variations.

1. non-linear porosity
2. directional porosity
3. closed cell foam

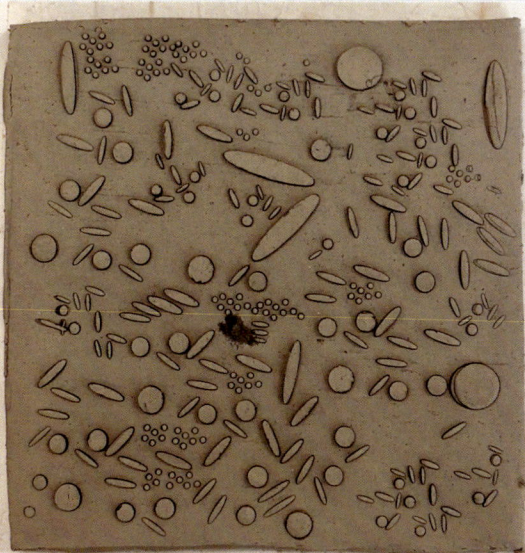

III. MACROCOSM AND MICROCOSM

The Great Cosmic Mountain at Borobudur in Java is meant to be a mirror of the cosmos, as depicted by Buddhists in the ninth century. In medieval Europe, each constellation of the zodiac was identified with a part of the human body, precisely linking human organs to the movement of the stars in the sky. This, according to Michel Foucault, was the era of similitudes, in which each aspect of life on earth was understood to mirror another in the cosmos, thereby acquiring larger meaning. This way of thinking is still present today, in projects such as Siamak Hariri's Bahá'í Temple, in Santiago, Chile.

Architecture as a microcosm reflects our place in the universe, and the projects in this theme demonstrate the endless varieties of this concept. It can be a monument which evokes a larger world, such as Étienne-Louis Boullée's imaginary Cenotaph for Newton or Erich Mendelsohn's Einstein tower built in Potsdam, Germany. Or it may, through its environmental systems, functionally become a small environment unto itself, such as Solsearch's Ark in Prince Edward Island. It may appear as a "living organism," integrated with the systems surrounding it and swaying with natural currents of air and heat while retaining its particularity, such as Diller Scofidio + Renfro's Blur Building on the shores of Lake Neuchâtel in Switzerland.

Lastly, textiles researcher and artist Carole Collet works with actual living organisms to develop new understandings of materials and to explore new formal possibilities for artists, designers, and architects. Her projects "Botanical Fur" and "Bio-lace" point the way to a dialogical design process, in which designer and matter itself are equal agents in the development of new art forms.

Opposite: National Spiritual Assembly of the Baháis of Chile.

DYMAXION HISTORIES:
SPACE, TIME, AND GEODESIC DOMES
John Turnbull

Across cultures and across time, people have wanted to make buildings with a sense of unity, in which one feels oriented to and aligned with all the known elements. This strand of organicism, this way of relating human life to the natural world through architecture, aims to curate the universe and can tell us about the scope of a culture's concerns and understanding. The geodesic dome is a twentieth-century, Western manifestation of this longing and embodies the burgeoning sense – partly a product of the space race and partly of social factors – of global interconnectedness, and the spirit of change of the late 1960s.

As scientific and cultural understandings of the universe and our place in it change over time and geography, our buildings have adapted to match. These projects act as landmarks in the taxonomy of the known, letting us find our bearings somewhere between the very small and the very large. Early Buddhist and Hindu temples were planned to reproduce in macrocosm the mandala, "a layered series of concentric geometric figures that served … for meditation," and itself a design which "represented cosmic order," a microcosm of the universe.[1]

After the discoveries of Copernicus rocked the Western understanding of our position in space, architect Étienne Boullée drew a Cenotaph for Newton in the 1780s that reflected this new, scientific world view; his design "projected the interior as the sphere of the planet and the exterior as the sphere of the universe, pierced with stars."[2] Likewise, the discovery of the theory of relativity in the early twentieth century led to the construction of the Einstein Tower in Potsdam, designed by Erich Mendelsohn between 1917 and 1920. Here architecture not only expresses a new scientific understanding of the world, but a dominant cultural movement, German expressionism, as well. The two merge and are held together in the building; it becomes a microcosm of a holistic world view. On the cultural context around the tower, Kathleen James writes that

> Relativity appeared to many among its lay audience, admirers and detractors alike, to be an irrational theory, and thus consistent with the growing appreciation of expressionism, whose literature, theatre, cinema, and art were now enjoyed by a far greater audience

than the Berlin and Munich café coteries engaged in their production before the war.[3]

Understandings of the natural and social worlds were resonating with one another and this resonance was reified through the design and construction of the tower, a monument to relativity.

With their grand debut at Expo 67 in Montreal, Buckminster Fuller's geodesic domes fit neatly into this history of organicism in architectural form. Both in terms of construction principles and aesthetic effects, the domes are a direct cultural encapsulation of Western society's self-orientation, in the late 1960s, within the great taxonomy of life, the universe, and everything. It was a time of expanding global consciousness and a questioning of entrenched belief systems and structures of all kinds.

Writing in the context of the strikes and demonstrations that took place in Paris in 1968, Johan Kugelberg recalls that

> The Chinese Cultural Revolution, the iconic Che Guevara, Castro, and above all the anti-Vietnam war movement inspired and influenced student activism globally. Left-wing groups flourished, with radical bookstores, pamphleteers, and community activism increasingly becoming a part of the everyday fabric of student life. Street protests become common throughout 1966 and 1967.[4]

Top to bottom: (1) "Cosmic Mountain," Borobodur, Java; (2) Cenotaph for Newton; (3) Einstein Tower, Potsdam, Germany

Left to right: (4) Earthrise as seen from Apollo 8, 1968; (5) Playing with the "Earth ball"

Also in 1968, the Apollo 8 mission sent back photographs of planet Earth; these images "established our planetary facthood and beauty and rareness and began to bend human consciousness."[5]

The geodesic dome as a design concept was widely seen as a representation of a dawning ecological consciousness: it looked like the planet, and this, combined with its property of being able to contain the maximum amount of space with the minimum amount of materials, spoke to a culture newly attuned to issues of global scarcity and resource distribution. It had a structure that embodied unity and interdependency — it was made of

> a multitude of short vectors which direct the flow of forces along a web of steel struts. … Without these forces being able to flow smoothly back and forth through hundreds of tetrahedrons – if, for example, there was a tear in the fabric mesh or a sudden obstruction in the system – the building would collapse. In other words, the flow of forces represents the life force of the dome.[6]

It was a symbol of life and worked on the principles of life. It was a symbol fit perfectly for its time. Guerrilla domes began to sprout up around America, including a "Drop City" built by young artists in Colorado. Macy and Bonnemaison quote "a late Dropper, Bill Voyd," recalling that

> We heard R. Buckminster Fuller lecture in Boulder, Colorado and decided to build domes. We had little building experience…. We learned how to scrounge materials, tear down abandoned buildings, use the unusable. … The garbage of America. Trapped inside a waste-economy man finds an identity as a consumer. Once outside the trap he finds enormous resources at his disposal – free… When one stops 'owning' things another can begin to use them. Energy is transformed, not lost.[7]

The anti-consumer sentiment of the Droppers, their desire to break out of a nationalistic identity and create a new one through new ways of building and living, meshed seamlessly with the spirit of the protesters on the other side of the ocean. Though not universally adopted by the global counterculture, the geodesic dome

(6) Buckminster Fuller, US Pavilion, Expo 67, Montreal, 1967

was in many ways the perfect symbol of its essential outlook. Its suitability to its ecological and counter-cultural moment helps to explain its popularity. It was the inspiration for a whole genre of build-your-own-dome books, read and followed by those who wanted to "fuse a sense of self with a sense of the cosmos."[8] What better expression of global unity and idealism than to "live lightly" in the image of the globe itself? In our climate of increasing nationalism, division, and environmental degradation, one wishes we could uncork the vigour, optimism, and sense of global responsibility embodied in Fuller's revolutionary design.

1   Richard Ingersoll and Spiro Kostof, *World Architecture: A Cross-Cultural History*. New York: Oxford University Press, 2013, 268.
2   Ingersoll and Kostof, *World Architecture*, 616.
3   Kathleen James, "Expression, Relativity, and the Einstein Tower," *Journal of the Society of Architectural Historians* 53, no. 4 (Dec 1994), 400.
4   Johan Kugelberg and Philippe Vermès, eds. *Beauty is in the Street: A Visual Record of the May '68 Paris Uprising*. London: Four Corners Books, 2011), 13.
5   Christine Macy and Sarah Bonnemaison, *Architecture and Nature: creating the American landscape*. New York: Routledge, 2003, 293.
6   Macy and Bonnemaison, *Architecture and Nature*, 309.
7   Macy and Bonnemaison, *Architecture and Nature*, 324.
8   Macy and Bonnemaison, *Architecture and Nature*, 329.

EXPLORATIONS IN ECOLOGICAL ARCHITECTURE: THE ARK ON PRINCE EDWARD ISLAND
Steven Mannell

Environmental architecture arrived in Canada in 1976 at a remote site in eastern Prince Edward Island, incongruously heralded by a pair of helicopters bearing Canadian Prime Minister Pierre Elliott Trudeau and PEI Premier Alex Campbell. The dignitaries were welcomed by a throng of alternative technology proponents, counterculture youth, and rural Islanders. An experimental demonstration of self-reliant ecological architecture, the Ark included a south-facing greenhouse and solar panels, with earth-sheltered clapboard volumes to the north; it evoked associations with various structures from space stations to old barns, aptly expressing the hybrid of advanced research and traditional common sense behind its vision of a self-sufficient, ecologically engaged family life. According to its designers:

> The Ark is an ecologically designed bioshelter powered and heated by the wind and sun. It houses a research laboratory, living unit, family garden and a small commercial greenhouse and fish farm. The structure is experimental, exploring new ideas in self-sufficiency, in biological systems, and in intensive food production. The ultimate goal is to create shelters that sustain and support their inhabitants.[1]

The stark contrast of the two sides of the building — glass to the south, solid sheds to the north — demonstrated the primary objectives of its forms: as much exposure as possible to the warmth and energy of the southern sun, and as much protection as possible from the cold north winds. The solar strategy of minimizing energy needs, and maximizing energy harvest, informed every design decision, from site strategy to building detail. The Ark nestled into the slope to reduce exposed surface area; its highly-insulated airtight walls and roof minimized heat losses; it was sheltered by an earth berm and tree plantings from the north wind.

Architectural form was intertwined with systems both physical – solar and wind energy – and biological – food production and waste management. In the Ark there was no simple distinction between the architectural environment and the activities within: solar energy simultaneously drove photosynthesis in the food crops and provided heat and ventilation of the surrounding greenhouse; the food-growing media of water and soil also stored heat for later exchange with the greenhouse space above; and waste from one system became feedstock for another — plant

cuttings fed the fish, while nutrient-rich water from the fish tanks irrigated the planters. Human inhabitants of the Ark — a family of four lived there for a year and a half — managed the interplay of systems, enjoying the harvest of food while contributing their own wastes as compost to the nutrient cycle. Only gray water from the sinks and laundry escaped the Ark cycle, flowing into a dry well on site. Though not much larger than a house, the Ark embodied ambitions to transform Canada's future away from consumerism and toward a "conserver society," a new domestic lifestyle outside the materialist economy.

Top: (1) The Ark in winter, c. 1977
Above: (2) The farmhouse-style dining table at the heart of the Ark

Trudeau's remarks at the opening celebrated the Ark's "new commitment to living lightly on the earth," giving official sanction to the ideas of an emerging environmental counterculture. The field of ecological design arose out of the optimistic pro-environmental mood surrounding the first Earth Day in 1970. It was spurred by the challenges identified at the 1972 United Nations Conference on the Human Environment in Stockholm, and built on the grassroots solutions proposed by the Appropriate Technology movement. When the 1973 oil crisis shook official confidence in the future of fossil-fueled growth, governments became interested and began to seek new sources of energy. In 1975, the federal and provincial

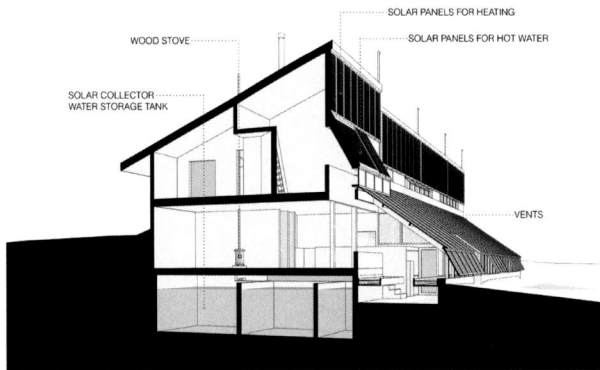

(3) Section through the Ark dwelling and kitchen greenhouse, showing the energy system

governments invited the New Alchemy Institute, a US-based collective of scientists and humanists whose goal was to "restore the lands, protect the seas, and inform the earth's stewards," to build a living demonstration of ecological architecture on a remote site in eastern Prince Edward Island. Funding and technical support came from federal agencies, while the Island provided the site at Spry Point and offered a hospitable policy environment with its commitment to alternative development pathways and a "small is beautiful" mindset.[2] David Bergmark and Ole Hammarlund of Solsearch Architects brought a synthesizing spatial vision to the assembly of techniques and ecosystems.

The Ark inspired further federal and provincial government efforts to encourage environmental design and renewable energy technologies, and by 1980 Canada was recognized internationally as a leader in the move towards a sustainable human environment. These environmental design approaches captured the popular imagination in Canada, and many important lessons were transferred from experimental projects to mainstream practices. During its short lifetime, thousands of people would visit the Ark, which functioned as both a research center and a demonstration project. Tourists and locals, architecture students, and appropriate technology advocates were drawn by the Ark's vision of a meaningful collaboration between humanity and nature. Later used as a fish hatchery, then as a community-run inn and restaurant, the Ark was demolished in 1999.[3]

1   Solsearch Architects, The PEI Ark poster, n.d [1976-1977].
2   E.F. Schumacher, *Small is Beautiful: Economics as if People Mattered*. New York: Harper and Row, 1973.
3   The text of this article is adapted from: Steven Mannell, *"Living Lightly on the Earth": Building an Ark for Prince Edward Island, 1974–76*. Halifax: Dalhousie Architectural Press, 2018.

(4) Section at Barn, Rockstorage and Greenhouse

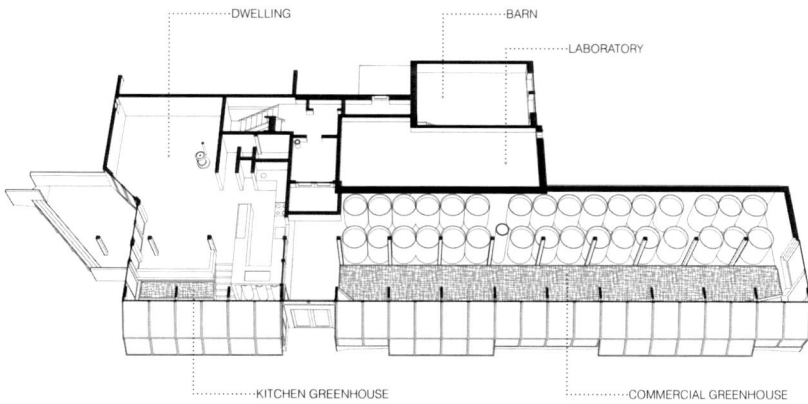

(5) Cutaway plan view of the main level of the Ark, indicating the major elements

PASSIVE SYSTEMS IN BUILDING DESIGN
Lucien Landry

In Europe and North America, the integration of passive environmental systems into large buildings is a recent trend. Yet people have been using passive design principles in vernacular architecture since they first started building. The thermal storage capacity of traditional earthen construction (such as adobe block or rammed earth), the wind-catching *bâdgir* of ancient Persia, the shaded tents of the Bedouin — all of these vernacular technologies show the ability of people from diverse cultures to observe how the Earth's natural weather systems work, and to harness these principles into their designs. Today, this work continues in the most technologically advanced buildings as well, such as Winnipeg's Manitoba Hydro Place, designed by the consortium of KPMB Architects, Smith Carter and Transolar (2009).

Bedouin tents and adobe buildings employ the thermal mass and air flow principles used in modern passive house construction (Figures 1 and 2). The Bedouin people bring only what they need as they travel through the harsh desert climate: their livestock, household goods, and tents. Their tents, woven of camel and goat wool, are made by the women of the community using an immense amount of embedded knowledge. The fabric provides shade from the unrelenting sun, protects inhabitants from sand storms, and provides warmth at night. Further analysis of the tents' construction reveals additional benefits: the use of black wool allows the sun to superheat the fabric surfaces to a temperature hotter than the surrounding air, causing an imbalance in pressure which forces the hot air inside the tent to rise, and allows cooler breezes to pass through. This strategy makes good use of natural airflow principles arising from the different thermal masses of landforms and bodies of water, creating winds that flow due to variations in temperature and pressure. The wool fabric also serves to protect against the occasional desert rain, swelling and closing off its pores when in contact with water, permitting the interior space to remain relatively dry.[1]

Vernacular earth building techniques also use airflow to maintain thermal comfort. As the sun heats the earthen mass of the structure, it causes hot air to rise and

Left to right: (1) Bedouin tents, 1912; (2) Adobe buildings, Acoma Pueble, 1938

allows for a breeze to flow throughout the space, helping to cool it during the day. At night, the heat absorbed by the adobe is released, warming the space and allowing for more energy to be absorbed the following day.[2] In both the tent and the adobe building, the use of natural materials and the embedded knowledge within them is essential to their thermal performance.

Passive House (*Passivhaus*) standards started as a conversation between engineer Bo Adamson of Lund University in Sweden, and physicist Wolfgang Feist of the Institute for Housing and the Environment in Germany in 1988; the concept has gained considerable traction over the decades.[3] Roberto Gonzalo and Rainer Vallentin describe Passive House techniques as a way of reducing the energy consumption of a building to such a low level that it hardly requires any mechanical heating, cooling, humidification or dehumidification sourced from external sources to satisfy comfort requirements.[4] Instead, the natural heating, cooling and thermal storage capacities of wind, sun, vegetation, and earth are incorporated into the building systems, significantly lowering energy demands (Figure 3).

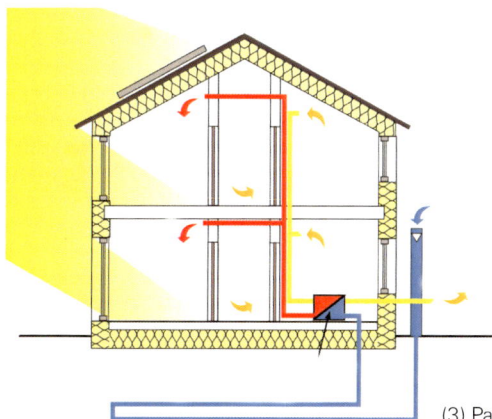

(3) Passive House principles

Left to right: (4) North (a) and South (b) facades; (5) Atrium. Opposite page: (6) Water feature; (7) Airflow diagram.

Since, ultimately, human comfort is the most important objective for designers, Passive House standards specify comfort levels for air temperatures of 18-24 °C, floor temperatures of 19-26 °C, and relative air humidity of 40-70%. These benchmarks vary with the seasons and climactic regions (e.g. arid, tropical, or polar), since different climates require specific solutions to achieve comfortable indoor environments.

The vernacular examples discussed earlier incorporate natural processes of energy storage and thermal flows using simple techniques, at small scales, and in ways that may not be immediately apparent. Modern buildings, by contrast, such as Winnipeg's Manitoba Hydro Place, also draw on natural systems to provide a framework for their passive system design strategies, but they do so more visibly. Hydro Place is a 22-storey, 64,500 sq ft office building. Thanks to the intelligent usage of its surrounding environmental context, the building uses 60-70% less energy than similarly sized office buildings, and maintains 100% fresh air throughout the building 365 days a year, a remarkable feat considering that Winnipeg has seasonal temperatures fluctuating between 30 °C and -30 °C.[5] To achieve low energy usage and continuous fresh air circulation, the design incorporates a wide range of passive systems (Figure 7), occasionally boosted by mechanical systems that operate on two separates modes: summer/shoulder season mode and winter mode. During the summer and shoulder seasons, air is drawn into the building through large operable windows within a double curtain wall system on the south façade (Figure 4a). The air is heated or cooled as needed, passed through raised floor plenums to regulate the temperature of adjacent spaces, and then exhausted through a 115m tall chimney to the north, using the stack effect (Figure 4b).

During the winter months, exterior air is drawn into the building mechanically and heated by geothermal ground lines. The chimney is closed, forcing warm, stale air down into the parkade, where it heats the space before passing through heat exchangers. If the air needs further conditioning, 22m tall waterfalls provide humidification or dehumidification as the air passes through them (Figures 6 and 7).

Passive systems, in both vernacular and contemporary architecture, enable people to be comfortable in the built environment. They draw on inexhaustible natural systems that are more sustainable and cleaner than mechanical systems powered by fossil fuels. Although the systems employed in vernacular buildings are simple in principle, they can be used and adapted to provide thermal comfort in complex projects such as Manitoba Hydro Place. Passive systems may be visually evident — such as a waterfall feature — or difficult to distinguish, as in the properties found within the Bedouin tents. Although these very different constructions have few evident similarities, they share the fundamental design principles of drawing from nature and taking advantage of the knowledge embedded in the materials chosen for construction. Regardless of the scale, program, or location of construction, the use of passive systems is beneficial and important in all architecture.

1   Shady Attia, "Assessing the Thermal Performance of Bedouin Tents in Hot Climates," 2014. https://orbi.uliege.be/bitstream/2268/164042/1/ID%2312530_Final2.pdf
3   Maria Luisa Parra-Saldivar and William Batty, "Thermal behaviour of adobe construction," *Building and Environment* 41, no. 12 (2006): 1892-1904.
3   Wolfgang Feist, (2014). *The world's first Passive House*, Darmstadt-Kranichstein, Germany. 10.13140/RG.2.1.4012.7526
4   Roberto Gonzalo and Rainer Vallentin, *Passive House Design: Planning and design of energy-efficient buildings*, Calbe: GCC Grafisches Centrum Cuno, 2014.
5   "Manitoba Hydro / KPMB Architects." *ArchDaily*. Accessed 9 Oct 2018. <https://www.archdaily.com/44596/manitoba-hydro-kpmb-architects/> ISSN 0719-8884

NON-ISOLATED THERMODYNAMIC MATERIALISM: JADE ECO PARK AND THE BLUR BUILDING
Andrew Falls

In 2013, Harvard University's Graduate School of Design hosted a symposium on "Thermodynamic Materialism." Led by the GSD's Green Design / Energy Environments and Design Lab, this symposium aimed to rethink architectural materiality through the lens of thermodynamics, and to consider the thermal qualities of a space as a key contributor to a building's design concept. One of the symposium's participants, Kiel Moe, has written a book further exploring ways architects approach thermal comfort — either insulating a space from its thermal flows (which he called "isolated thermodynamics"), or not ("non-isolated thermodynamics").[1] In the realm of non-isolated thermodynamic materialism, architecture is concerned with more than the tectonic arrangement of materials — it positions itself within a holistic planetary view, considering natural forces as governing processes. Here, according to Moe, buildings are understood as "non-isolated, transient structures of dissipation," where their microcosmic relation to the macrocosm of nature is that of a harmony between climactic modifications and constantly fluctuating atmospheric processes.

Philippe Rahm calls surfaces "inherently non-organic,"[2] citing early humans' original dwellings as microclimates within caves. In his view, the main purpose of architecture is to create a desirable climate for human occupation, which does not necessarily require a distinct delineation between interior and exterior space. Rahm's most ambitious work to date is Taichung Central Park (also known as Jade Eco Park) — designed with landscape architect Catherine Mosbach and architect Ricky Liu and Associates — which is nearing completion in Taiwan. Rahm's vision for the park is to "give back the outdoors to the inhabitants and visitors by proposing to create exterior spaces where the excesses of the subtropical warm and humid climate of Taichung are lessened."[3]

The conceptual drawings for the park highlight, in pastel colours, a gradient of climate modification devices that augment the natural microclimates of the site (Figure 1). At each point in the park, there is no moment that tries to create a false sense of static atmospheric equilibrium; instead, the park welcomes the reality

(1) Concept drawing for Jade Eco Park (Central Park, Taichung)

of spatial experience as a gradient of varying phenomena. This gradient is a result of three factors: the level of pollution (noise, chemical, and pest), temperature, and humidity. The physical relationship of these spatial inputs creates spaces that "overlap, separate, regroup, densify, dilute, generating a variety of atmospheres where the users can choose and appropriate as they see fit."[4] These created atmospheres are not unique to the park, but mimic those that occur naturally throughout the Earth, making each moment a microcosmic imitation of the macrocosm of atmospheric nature.

The competition drawings for the park provide an insight into the team's organicist ideologies, as does the naming of each climatic modification device after a naturally-occuring atmospheric process. For example, the convective cooling device is named "Anticyclone" after a cold pressure system, while the evaporative cooling device is named "Stratus Cloud" after the phase change from liquid to gas that occurs when clouds are formed through evaporation (Figure 3). The naming of these devices gives us insight into the designers' intent of harnessing natural phenomena in a designed landscape, situating the work in an organicist framework.

Diller, Scofidio + Renfro's Blur Building was also developed around a naturally-occurring atmospheric phenomenon. An ephemeral media pavilion built for the 2002 Swiss Expo on the shores of Lake Neuchâtel, this project "read" the fluctuating climatic conditions of the lake to generate varying intensities of water vapour. The result was "sculpted" weather, a blurred, "decidedly low-definition" space that welcomed its visitors to inhabit a gradient of vapour, rather than a defined enclosure.[5] Blur's varying meteorological input created a sense of harmony with its aquatic context by actively responding to it while, similarly to Taichung Central Park, eschewing any deceptive sense of stability. Architecture that situates itself as a microcosm within the atmosphere must celebrate changeability, or it would have to reject the realities of the constant flow of atmospheric processes. In *Essays on Thermodynamics, Architecture and Beauty*, Iñaki Abalos suggests that by allowing for these fluctuations, architecture can aim for a "momentary attainment

(2) "Stratus Cloud" weather-making device; (3) Phillippe Rahm in the park, 2018

of structures and regimes of a higher order and inner stability, […] linked to the exchange of matter, energy and information."[6]

Clearly, both Blur and Taichung Central Park — despite lacking evident architectonic order — possess a highly ordered idea of harmony, one which is predicated on the greater order of the Earth's natural processes. Alberti emphasizes such harmony when he writes "what is needed is a regulating factor, and that is concinnitas, by which unity and therefore beauty are achieved."[7] Blur's order is perhaps not visually graspable, but its representation of flow is its "regulating factor."

While the Blur Building repesents a state of harmony with the lake, the Taichung garden presents multiple and varied experiences of harmonious flux. The resulting experience is similar to musical polyphony, which van Eck calls "a harmony of contrasting qualities – such as the high and low pitch voices."[8] Here, instead of encountering a variety of sounds, the visitor experiences a variety of climatic outputs, both artificially constructed and naturally occurring, which create a multitude of sensory impressions. Perhaps at these moments, one may sense thermal resonance similar to the feeling of hearing a well-written piece of wwwmusic — a harmony that results from the dynamic and subjective dialogue between varying atmospheric qualities and the person experiencing them.

In discussing the idea of microcosm in organicism, Mari Hvattum says it "becomes synonymous with a self-regulating organic system: the organic system is a 'little world,' by virtue of its self-referentiality."[9] This idea of a self-regulating microcosm may be central to thermodynamic materialism in architecture. The projects presented here express and celebrate gradient and entropy, and demonstrate a careful integration with their microclimactic contexts and macroclimactic processes. They indicate that to achieve harmony with nature's climate systems, architects must accept that they are in constant flux. This approach contradicts any idea of dominating nature, instead emphasizing our subjection to it, and reorienting architecture towards natural phenomena.

(4) Diller, Scofidio + Renfro, Blur Building, Yverdon-les-Bains, Switzerland

1   Kiel Moe, *Insulating Modernism: Isolated and Non-isolated Thermodynamics in Architecture*. Basel: Birkhauser, 2014.
2   Philippe Rahm Architects, "Domestic Astronomy." Accessed October 06, 2018. http://www.philipperahm.com/data/projects/domesticastronomy/index.html.
3   Philippe Rahm Architects, "Jade Eco Park." Accessed October 06, 2018. http://www.philipperahm.com/data/projects/taiwan/index.html.
4   Catherine Mosbach, Phillipe Rahm, and Ricky Liu. "The Taichung Gateway Park Competition – Projects of the Winners," 2012. Accessed July 4, 2012. http://elap.es/archpapers/2012/03/the-taichung-gateway-parkcompetition-projects-of-the-winners/
5   Diller, Scofidio + Renfro, "Blur Building." Accessed October 06, 2018. https://dsrny.com/project/blur-building.
6   Iñaki Abalos and renata Snetkiewicz. *Abalos and Snetkiewicz: Essays on Thermodynamics, Architecture and Beauty,* ed. Lluís Ortega (New York: Actar D, 2015)
7   Leon Battista Alberti in Caroline van Eck, *Organicism in Nineteenth Century Architecture, an enquiry into its theoretical and philosophical background*. Amsterdam: Architecture et Natura Press, 1994.
8   Caroline van Eck, *Organicism in Nineteenth Century Architecture, an enquiry into its theoretical and philosophical background*. Amsterdam: Architecture et Natura Press, 1994.
9   Mari Hvatti, "'Unfolding from Within:' Modern Architecture and the Dream of Organic Totality." *Journal of Architecture* 11, 2006: 497-509.

MACROCOSM AND MICROCOSM

BIOMIMICRY IN CONTEMPORARY ARCHITECTURE
Liam Logan

"Organicism in architecture," according to Caroline van Eck,

> is a constantly shifting pattern of thought, opinions and arguments, which has a common element in the preoccupation with the relation between the organic in architecture and nature, expressed in the metaphorical application to architectural concepts used to describe organic nature.[1]

For centuries, the philosophy of organicism has been used in architecture to justify symmetry and hierarchy in plan and elevation design, and to develop architectural ornamentation. It was commonplace for architects to incorporate natural motifs or patterns in their works. But in 1968, a significant transformation took place in people's understanding of their relationship to the natural world. The spark was an image from Apollo 8, received and circulated around the globe — according to Christine Macy and Sarah Bonnemaison, "the vision of the Earth as a planet in space became an icon for the emerging ecology movement."[2] As global pollution and natural resource depletion continued into the 21st century, environmental sustainability became a major concern for architects. With widespread acknowledgment of the undeniable fact that we are a microcosm in the macrocosm of the universe, a growing environmental consciousness propelled the evolution of organicism from the metaphorical application of expressing nature through architecture to the contemporary practice of building in an environmentally sustainable manner.

One strategy used to aid environmentally sustainable design is biomimicry. Nature has provided inspiration to architects throughout history, for the aesthetics of a building's form and decoration. Biomimicry in contemporary architecture shifts the focus; according to Michael Pawlyn, it is "design inspired by the way functional challenges have been solved in biology"[3] (Figure 1). It embodies van Eck's option "to characterize the role of organicism in terms of strategy, since a strategy is a well-considered consequent course of action or thought to reach a well-defined goal."[4] We see this in biomimicry, as it seeks solutions for human challenges by emulating nature's principles and strategies. But why is biomimicry only now

Left to right: (1) Biomimicry: Shoot and Norman Foster's "Gherkin," London; (2) The Eden Project, Cornwall

becoming so prominent? "While fascination with nature undoubtedly goes back as long as human existence itself, now we can revisit the advances in biology with the massive advantages of expanding scientific knowledge"[5] and technology that was once unimaginable. One example is the electron microscope, which allows us to study nature and living organisms on a molecular level. Biomimicry advances nature-inspired architecture as a

> 'strategy' rather than 'theory.' [This] highlights the concrete and specific or applied character of the use of organic metaphors: they were not part of a body of general and normative principles … but received their particular formulation and meaning in the attempt to arrive at the solution of a particular problem.[6]

Grimshaw Architects' Eden Project in Cornwall exemplifies the practices through which biomimicry is translated to architecture (Figure 2). As one of the world's largest plant enclosures, its particular challenge was to be built in the lightest and most ecological way possible, although the construction took five years (from 1996-2001).[7]

The site was a china clay (kaolinite) quarry, which presented the challenge of designing a structure that could easily adapt to changes in the ground level. From the beginning, the design team looked to nature for a solution appropriate to the program and site, seeking, as Goethe advised, "to understand the laws of growth and form in organic nature."[8] They found their answer in soap bubbles, noticing that as the diameter of each bubble expands, it grows in height. Adapting this principle to the quarry site, the designers permitted each bubble to be sufficiently large to accommodate the plants inside, and then strung the bubbles together along the uneven ground terrain (Figure 5).

The next challenge was to create a structural system that would be as light as possible, with a method similar to van Eck's "systematic analysis in structural terms of the way in which architectural forms are developed in accordance with the methods of nature,"[9] the Eden Project's design team studied a series of "carbon

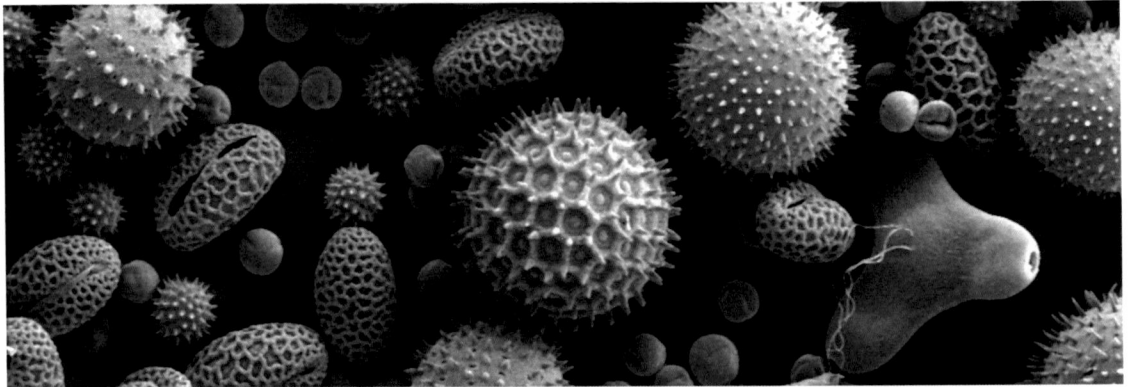

(3) Electron micrograph of pollen from common plants.

molecules and radiolaria through to pollen grains. This study revealed that the most effective way of structuring a spherical form is with the geodesic arrangement of pentagons and hexagons that was first pioneered by Buckminster Fuller"[10] (Figure 3).

The next step was to "right-size" the pentagons and hexagons, to maximize sun penetration with the least amount of structure. As glass would be a large constant due to its weight and structural integrity, the team instead used a high-strength polymer, ethylene tetrafluoroethylene (ETFE), in tension rather than compression or bending. This use of tension was something Grimshaw Architects was previously aware of, as a biological solution seen in nature to form cell membranes and spider webs (Figure 4).

The use of biomimicry throughout the Eden Project's design resulted in an eco-friendly and sustainable project. Combining billions of years of nature's development with the scientific advances of today, biomimicry emulates natural methods to create better designs — which, in contemporary architecture, means a focus on environmental sustainability, thus creating a better harmony between the built environment and nature.

1   Caroline van Eck, *Organicism in Nineteenth-century Architecture: an Inquiry into Its Theoretical and Philosophical Background*. Amsterdam: Architectura et Natura Press, 1994, 25.
2   Christine Macy and Sarah Bonnemaison, *Architecture and Nature: Creating the American Landscape*. London; New York: Routledge, 2003, 293.
3   Michael Pawlyn, *Biomimicry in Architecture* (2nd ed.), Newcastle: RIBA, 2016, 1.
4   van Eck, *Organicism*, 27.
5   Pawlyn, *Biomimicry*, 1.
6   van Eck, *Organicism*, 27.
7   Hugh Pearman, *Equilibrium: The Work of Nicholas Grimshaw & Partners*, Singapore: Phaidon, 2000, 116.
8   van Eck, *Organicism*, 105.
9   van Eck, *Organicism*, 142.
10 Pawlyn, *Biomimicry*, 38.

Above: (4) Panorama of The Eden Project
Below: (5) Grimshaw Architects, Poster of The Eden Project showing quarry, sectional and planimetric views

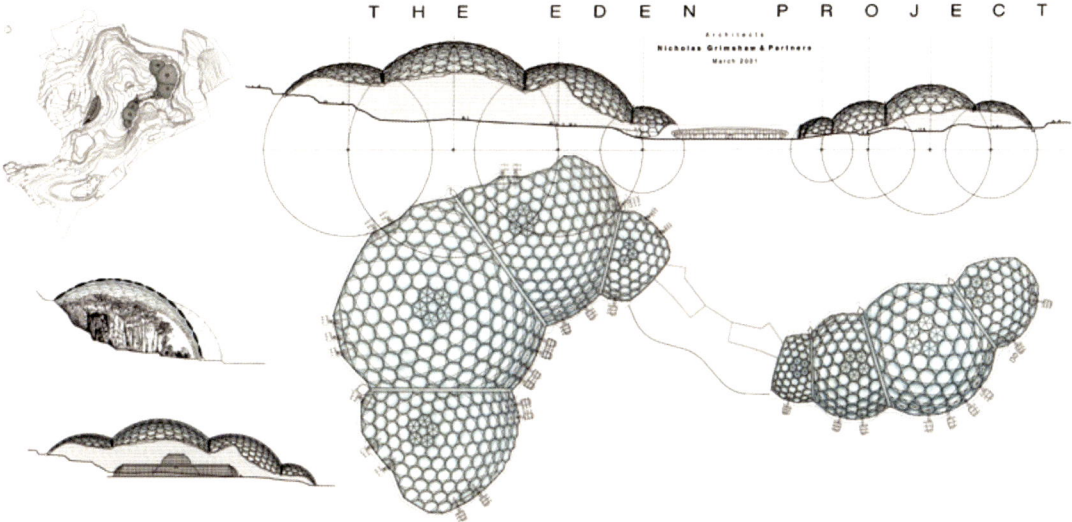

THE EDEN PROJECT

Architects
Nicholas Grimshaw & Partners
March 2001

BOTANICAL FUR
Carole Collet

The textile and plant worlds have been intrinsically linked throughout our history. Deriving materials, threads, and fabrics from plants such as cotton, flax, or even agave and tree bark has been historically linked to our evolution and ability to transform our environment to evolve a purpose-built everyday materiality. Equally, the manipulation of plant architecture is linked to our agricultural and horticultural history, where intersecting species and breeding techniques have led to the ongoing and competitive development of new plant cultivars. While the production of fibres and cloth, and the development and control of plant systems, provide rich contexts of reference, the current ecological paradigm sets a new scene to research and prototype original textile constructs that are mindful of our limited natural resources.

The Botanical Fur research project is an enquiry into the plasticity and morphogenetic control of fur-like botanical systems and is concerned primarily with plants' ability to grow fur. Whether located on roots, stems, or leaves, trichomes (i.e. plant hairs) provide a range of functions such as defence against pests, adaptation to temperature and climate change, protection, and biosensing. While these biological functions are a result of evolution,

> new insights are emerging on fundamental aspects of the plasticity development – a phenomenon unique to plants and therefore chartering new territory not encountered in animal or microbial systems.[1]

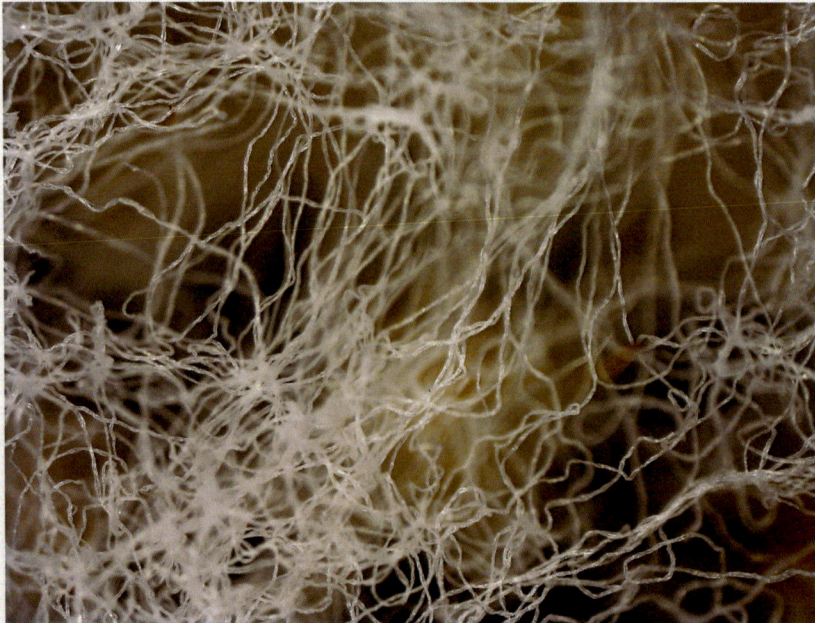

The project asks: what can we learn from plants' fur systems that can inform new textile fabrication methods? Can we harvest plant fur for biofabrication purposes? Can we genetically control the mechanics and architecture of plants roots and trichomes to grow textiles? This research project explores biological functions in plant systems to prototype new textile conceptual constructs and new material assembly techniques. The project is structured around three phases of research. The first phase sets out to explore the plasticity and tactility of natural plant fur, such as that produced by *Cephalocereus senilis*, a species of cactus originating from Mexico, to create a range of miniature fur textile samples. The second phase of the project intersects plant tissue engineering techniques with textile patterning methods to grow textile-like root assemblies *in vitro*. The final phase (pending funding) will research plant synthetic biology techniques to control the characteristics of root hair and colour. The first and second phases will be presented at the exhibition "Les Fabriques du Vivant" at the Pompidou Centre in 2019.

---

1   Colin Turnbull, ed. "Plant Architecture and its manipulation," *Annual Plant Reviews* 17, Blackwell (2005): 13.

Left to right: (1) *Epostoa melanostele*; (2) *Oreocereus doelziannus*; (3) *Mamillaria plumosa*

IV. GEOMETRIES DERIVED FROM NATURE

Design has long drawn inspiration from natural geometries, and many advances in architecture have relied on observational interpretation of natural phenomena. The Arab culture invested their faith by transcribing the geometrical perfection they saw in nature into architecture — from the grandiose spiral minaret of the Great Mosque of Samarra to the intricate tile work and muquarnas in the Alhambra Palace in Granada. In European Gothic cathedrals, we can still see rose windows which give materiality to the immaterial light of the divine; the magnificent Mughal gardens and palaces were based on Persian geometric models, such as we see in the Safavid-era Sheikh Lotfollah Mosque of Isfahan.

The shift from a religious conception of geometry to a scientific one is really a shift from an idea of geometric perfection (think of the Platonic solids) to an idea — largely argued by Goethe — of representing the patterns of organic growth as a meaningful foundation for architecture. This inspired architects such as Henri Labrouste to combine observation of plants with a new rational use of materials, resulting in logical and progressive buildings. This was the era of ever-larger iron and glass enclosures for railway stations and civic buildings.

Organicism is not only a strategy for design, it is also a method to invent new ways of building. D'Arcy Thompson insisted that mathematical geometry could explain growth patterns in living nature. Now a century old, his book *On Growth and Form* influenced a generation of engineers and architects, such as Robert Le Ricolais, Anne Tyng, and Haresh Lalvani. The pursuit of lightweight structures through the study of spider webs and the minimal surfaces of single-celled organisms can be charted through Frei Otto's tensile structures and the sweeping surfaces of Zaha Hadid; their work is the result of the observation of natural elements, abstracted into organized and rationalized geometrical experiments.

This understanding of the relationship between physical forces, natural growth and geometric form has greatly influenced contemporary designers and architects, as they use computational tools to accelerate the iterative calculations involved in form-finding that includes multiple design parameters. Jenny Sabin Studio's "Lumen" installation in the courtyard of MoMA PS1 project "closes the loop" between fabric structures and geometric tiling, as she brings this work into three dimensions.

Opposite: Dome, Sheikh Lotfollah Mosque, Isfahan, 1619

SCIENTIFIC ORGANICISM:
THE BIBLIOTHÈQUE SAINTE-GENEVIÈVE
Katie Kirkpatrick

Design has long sought inspiration from nature, which has informed everything from decorative pattern to structural materials. The geometries found in nature have provided architectural inspiration for the ninth-century tile patterns found in Granada's Alhambra and for the Gothic rose window of Chartres Cathedral. In 19th-century France, this long-standing association took a new form, when an emphasis on empirical research and functionality gave a new order to the biological world and offered a new direction for Western architecture. This new direction, scientific organicism, is expressed in Henri Labrouste's Bibliothèque Sainte-Geneviève, where his awareness of ongoing scientific debates resulted in a building that combines rationality, innovative use of materials and expression of program into logical and progressive architecture.

Scientific discovery experienced tremendous advancement in the 19th century, when gradual movement away from philosophical and religious understandings of the natural world gave way to empirical research driven by observation and critical study.[1] While Charles Darwin's evolutionary theory dominates the century's scientific discourse, the groundwork for his discovery was laid decades earlier by early biologists like Jean-Baptiste Lamarck, whose systematic studies resulted in the field's initial system of classifying living things. An ardent critic of Lamarck was Georges Cuvier, whose own work expanded on Linnaean taxonomy, allowing both fossils and living species to be classified with greater specificity (Figure 1). In 1830, Cuvier engaged in a series of debates against Etienne Geoffroy Saint-Hilaire on the topic of "whether the forms of organisms are determined by their function – the position defended by Cuvier – or whether all organic forms can be deduced from one basic type, regardless of their function – the view held by Geoffroy."[2] The winner of the debates is subjective and the details stray from architectural relevance but, as Caroline van Eck notes, "the debate is important because it offers a very clear insight into the slow transformation from Aristotelian notions of purposive unity into Darwinian notions of functionality."[3]

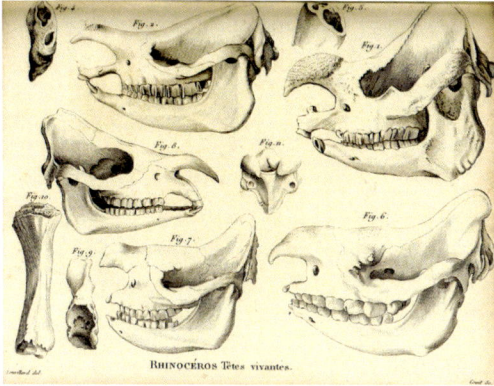

Left to right: (1) Cuvier, *Research into the fossilized bones of quadrapeds*; (2) Bibliothèque Sainte-Geneviève, Paris

19th century developments in science resonated far beyond their original fields; Cuvier and Geoffroy's debates on comparative anatomy and the relationship between form and function captured the attention of many architects in the 1830s. Lèon Vaudoyer was inspired to find fundamental similarities between the natural and man-made environments, developing the principle that the same conditions determining the functional integrity of an organism governed buildings."[4] For Labrouste, scientific developments shaped his view that architecture is "a complete organism, in which structure, materials, and configuration all led to a completeness."[5]

While in his early twenties, Labrouste won the Grand Prix, and the resulting time spent studying in Rome had long-lasting impacts on him. He formed strong working relationships with Vaudoyer and others; their group became known as the "Romantic Pensionnaires," and together they developed their own method of architectural study. By studying archaeological sites alongside ancient ruins, the group began to look at architecture not as static perfection but rather as something which evolved over time and was embedded with legible traces of change. This led to careful investigations into materials and proportions, "underscoring the relationship between form and its material support."[6] Throughout the course of their work, the Cuvier-Geoffroy debate and biological thought had influence on the Pensionnaires, Labrouste included; architecture could be studied and classified similarly to the living world, and it should also reflect the changes and developments of the society that had created it.[7]

Labrouste's Bibliothèque Sainte-Geneviève may be considered one of the first buildings designed with the influence of such formal scientific guidance. The library, part of Paris's Sorbonne University, was designed and built between 1839 and 1852. From the exterior, the building is a simple oblong box, with rhythmic partially blind arcades and minimal decoration (Figure 2). The Bibliothèque's exterior references the classical traditions still popular at the time but also hints that it belongs to something different. For example, classical tradition dictates that the ends and

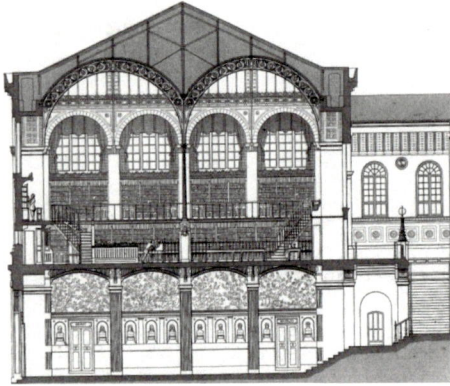
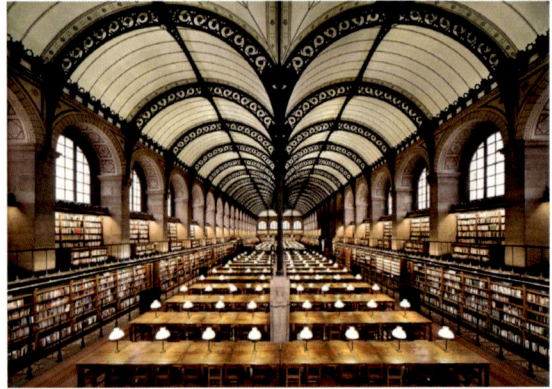

Left to right: (3) Section; (4) Reading room

centre of the façade should be strongly emphasized but the Bibliothèque's are not; Bressani and Grignon note that "Labrouste clearly wished to blur any overt reference to classical types that would normally have been used for the design of a civic building such as a library."[8]

Labrouste constructed a narrative that is evident in the Bibliothèque's architecture. Visitors begin on the street, part of the outside world and removed from knowledge. They process through the vestibule, along the compressed ground floor and up the staircase to the reading room, whose high ceilings, natural light and highly visible book storage indicate one's arrival in a place dominated by learning and higher truth (Figure 3).[9] The reading room is defined by its exposed iron structure, where slender, double-barrel vaulted iron frames rest on traditional masonry piers (Figure 4). Around the perimeter, bookcases step up on two levels, filling the perimeter arches. Large clerestory windows above allow natural light to filter in. Floral motifs carved into the ironwork (Figure 5) speak directly to natural inspiration; that this decoration is incorporated into slender tree-like columns is especially fitting.

Walter Curt Behrendt identified Labrouste's use of iron as a "hidden source of modernism," noting that the Bibliothèque Sainte-Geneviève was the first building to use the material on such a scale. He described it as courageous and "a true representative of that new spirit which thinks first of the organism of each structure."[10] Labrouste was also one of the first to incorporate the use of gas lighting into architectural design, and used it as a tool to influence the sensory experience of being in the library.[11] As well, the combination of traditional masonry with exposed, innovative structure and innovative technology speaks to the building's biological influences – it contains traces of its ancestry while reflecting the society for which it was created.

Labrouste's library was built at a time when rational thought and scientific discovery were helping give shape to the now-established disciplines of science and

Clockwise, from above: (5) Detail of the iron roof trusses; (6) Bibliothèque Nationale de France XXIII, 1998. © Candida Höfer/SOCAN (2019); (7) Sagrada Familia.

architecture; fittingly, it was also built at a time of similar developments in modern library science. Bibliothèque Sainte-Geneviève expresses so many of the values of the time, with the prioritization of cultivating, sharing and cataloguing knowledge chief among them.[12] Labrouste's interpretation of organicism was carried forward into his later Bibliothèque Nationale (Figure 6), and can even be seen in Antoni Gaudi's Sagrada Familia (Figure 7), where traditional Catholic church architecture is both respected and reimagined through innovation and natural inspiration.

1   Caroline van Eck, *Organicism in Nineteenth Century Architecture: an Enquiry into its Theoretical and Philosophical Background*, Amsterdam: Architectura et Natura Press, 1994, 214.
2   van Eck, *Organicism*, 216.
3   van Eck, *Organicism*, 219.
4   van Eck, *Organicism*, 221.
5   Corinne Belier, Barry Bergdoll and Marc Le Coeur, *Henri Labrouste: Structure Brought to Light*. New York: Museum of Modern Art, 2012, 69.
6   Belier, *Structure*, 58-59.
7   van Eck, *Organicism*, 226.
8   Martin Bressani and Marc Grignon, "Henri Labrouste and the Lure of the Real: Romanticism, Rationalism and the Bibliothèque Sainte-Geneviève," *Art History* 28, no. 5 (2005): 721.
9   Bressani and Grignon, "Labrouste and the Lure of the Real", 720.
10 Belier, *Structure*, 30.
11 Belier, *Structure*, 22.
12 Belier, *Structure*, 22.

FREI OTTO'S GERMAN PAVILION AT EXPO 67
Megan Burt

The German engineer and architect Frei Otto (1925-2015) was the inventor of contemporary tensile structures and founder of the Institute of Lightweight Structures in Stuttgart. He was greatly influenced by the philosophy of organicism; continually inspired by the forms and processes of nature, he sought to uncover the principles of minimal surfaces in spiderwebs and soap films, diatoms, and plant growth.

Caroline van Eck claims there are two varieties of organicism: the first outlines the relation between nature and art as expressed through imitation as ornament, while the second can only be attained when the exact methods and procedures of nature have been observed, examined, and abstracted so as to understand that aspect of organic unity,

> in a continuing quest for architectural form that cannot rest content with passive imitation of past forms. From this point of view, too, nature is seen as a provider of solutions for the problems of the aesthetic representation of tectonics.[1]

In other words, architects can learn by studying natural phenomena, and abstracting principles from them, to develop innovative solutions. This is what Frei Otto and the Institute for Lightweight Structures (IL) do.[2] Otto called his approach the "Reverse Path" method — through this method, he and his team at the IL studied formation processes in animate and inanimate nature, to understand the relationship between natural forces and what is formed. In this way, the observation of spiderwebs produced insight into the design of hanging tensile structures; soap bubbles informed the design of pneumatic structures; and so forth.

Otto's work first gained international attention with his design for the German pavilion at Expo 67 in Montreal. This project exemplifies Otto's observations of organic nature in his design process, and his use of "form-finding" to develop the required geometry. Van Eck sees form-finding as central to the historical development of architectural tectonics:

> In this orientation towards *Formerfindung* [form finding], Schinkel's tectonic approach to architecture clearly announces the science of tectonics as it was

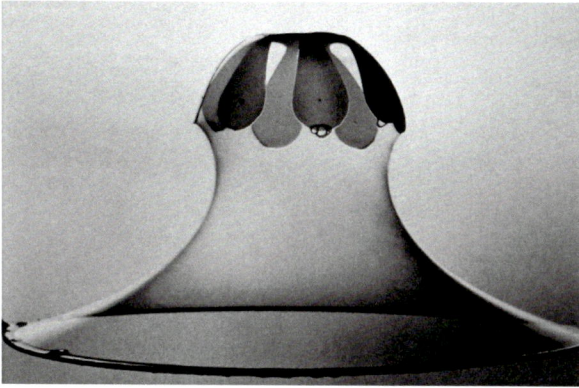

100 DEUTSCHLAND

FREI OTTO · DEUTSCHER PAVILLON MONTREAL

Wir suchen jene Baukunst, die aufgrund ähnlicher Prozesse entsteht, wie die Konstruktionen der Natur.

Left to right: (1) Soap film study; (2) Postage stamp depicting the German Pavilion from Expo 67

developed from the 1840s onwards by his student Bötticher, in which organicism plays a more prominent role than in the later stages of Schinkel's career.[4]

For the IL, form finding required them to observe the geometry of the natural world, quantify it mathematically, abstract its principles, replicate its dynamics in model form, and then scale up these models to develop designed and engineered structures. The larger goal, for Otto and his team, was to integrate architecture with the "ecological system of the earth's surface"[5] — making structures that were lighter, more energy-savvy, more adaptable, and more natural, without sacrificing safety and security.

By establishing this manifesto, Otto stressed the importance of the word "construction."[6] For him, "construction means bringing things together, building them. All material objects are constructions," and furthermore, all natural objects are also constructions, and should be observed for their self-formation processes.[7] By observing natural constructions — whether made by inanimate nature, animate nature, and/or animal and human technologies — architects may derive principles from these processes and apply them to the construction of new built forms.[8]

The Reverse Path method was of fundamental importance to the IL; through it, members began to recognize and understand the formation processes of inanimate and animate nature. By modelling natural constructions, they understood the forms that resulted from forces, and could develop the mathematics that allowed for both architectural form-making and structural engineering. One innovative building type pioneered and advanced by this method was the pneumatic construction. The IL's study of hydrostatic structure in cells allowed them to reverse-engineer surface tension in such structures, leading to their designs and engineering for large-scale pneumatic structures.[9]

Another productive set of experiments involved the use of soap film to study minimal areas for both tension-loaded membranes and rope/chain networks. It is known that soap-film membranes form when a closed frame made of wire or thread

(3) German Pavilion at Expo 67, Montréal.

is dipped into the liquid and removed (Figure 1). The observation that the membrane always contracts to the minimal possible surface, and that this surface holds with equal tension everywhere, led the IL to realize that this natural construction had a mathematical formulation. As Menges writes, they are "prestressed, flexurally nonrigid and plane load-bearing constructions that are nevertheless tension loaded."[10] These same qualities are true of tent structures, which led Otto to use the form-finding models as analogies for tent and net structures (Figure 2).[11]

The German Pavilion for Montreal's Expo 67 was a rope net tensile structure. In developing this design, Otto studied spider webs, explored the relationship between single membrane structures and rope nets, and assessed different means of rope net constructions (Figure 3). Upon the announcement of the 1965 competiton for the German Pavilion, Otto submitted his design, won the competition, and began 13 months of intensive design.

(4) Tensile roof detail, Munich Olympic Stadium, 1972

At that time, Otto understood that single- and double-curved surfaces could be formed with even-meshed nets if the angles were changeable at the nodes, rope nets being an extremely efficient spanning system. The nets were prefabricated in strips for ease of transportation and assembly, making the manufacture, installation, and erection extremely efficient. Once on the site, the strips were assembled on the ground and hoisted up the steel masts. To avoid the need for scaffolding, Otto designed the mesh with a 50cm interval between each cable, so construction workers could stand on the net without falling through.[12]

The 15m-wide mesh strips were made of 12mm steel rope. The entire net was supported by eight high and three low masts ranging between 14 and 36m in height. The entire structure covered 8,000 m², with a PVC-coated polyester membrane suspended 50cm below the net to provide shelter against weather. The success of this pavilion gained Otto the commission, in 1968, to design the Munich Stadium for the 1972 Olympic Games (Figures 4 and 5).[13]

Otto's exploration into the architectural and structural possibilities of animate and inanimate nature, and his development of methodologies for the observation of self-formation processes, continue to be valuable to architectural designers, engineers, biologists, and mathematicians. By providing opportunities to explore surface tension through his soap-film experiments, and by engaging in multiple other experiments through the Reverse Path method, Otto and his team at the IL explained many processes that were not previously understood or even studied. His translation of soap-film models into high-profile buildings, and his leading-edge engineering, carried out in collaboration with Ove Arup and Ted Happold, paved the way for subsequent computational design, from parametric design to emergent architecture.

1   Caroline van Eck, *Organicism in Nineteenth Century Architecture: an enquiry into its theoretical and philosophical background*. Amsterdam: Architectura et Natura Press, 1994, 162.
2   Axel Menges, *Frei Otto, Bodo Rasch: Finding Form*, *Towards an Architecture of the Minimal*. Deutscher Werkbund Bayern, 1995, 13.
4   van Eck, *Organicism*, 162.
5   Menges, *Finding Form*, 13.
6   Menges, *Finding Form*, 15.
7   Menges, *Finding Form*, 23.
8   Menges, *Finding Form*, 41.
9   Menges, *Finding Form*, 45.
10 Menges, *Finding Form*, 58.
11 Frei Otto and Marc Saugey's "Neige et Rocs" pavilion for the Swiss Regional Expo in Lausanne (1964) represented an important transition from tent to net structures, with the introduction of a reinforced PVC-net beneath the cotton membrane.
12 Menges, *Finding Form*, 94.
13 Menges, *Finding Form*, 106.

(5) Olympic Stadium, Munich, 1972.

LUMEN
Jenny Sabin Studio

Lumen,[1] the largest knitted architectural installation ever erected, is comprised of over a million yards of yarn to create a multisensory environment that responds to visitors, heat, and sunlight. Two lightweight fabric canopy structures made of tubular and cellular components employ recycled textiles, photo-luminescent and solar active yarns, to absorb and store UV energy, change color, and emit light, supported by three tensegrity towers and the surrounding courtyard walls. The winner of MoMA's 2017 Young Architects Program, it was installed in the courtyard of MoMA PS1 in Long Island City in the summer of 2017. This environment provided a welcome respite from a New York summer, as a built-in misting system activated by visitors humidified fabric stalactites to produce a refreshing micro-climate.

The project was designed using form-finding simulations informed by parameters such as sun, site, materials, program, and the material morphology of knitted cellular components. Resisting a biomimetic approach, Lumen employs an analogic design process where complex material behavior and processes are integrated with personal engagement and diverse programs.

(1) Aerial view of Lumen at PS1, Long Island City, 2017

High performance textiles are commonplace in the aerospace, automobile, sports, and marine industries, but architecture has yet to take full advantage of these. In the design process as well textiles offer architecture a robust platform for computational techniques, pattern manipulation, pre-programmed material production, and fabrication to become part of an interconnected design loop.[2] Over the last decade, knitting has begun to be explored at an architectural scale; since the *myThread* pavilion in 2012, Jenny Sabin Studio has explored generative design and digital fabrication in knitted multi-sensory responsive environments.[3] Lumen builds on six years of design research at the intersections of knitted textiles, biology, computation, and architecture, as well as the work of others such as Sean Ahlquist; Mette Ramsgard Thomsen and her colleagues at the Centre for Information Technology and Architecture (CITA), Royal Danish Academy of Fine Arts; and Jane Scott.[4]

Technical files for the digital knit production of each part of the installation were used to program the Shima Seiki's WHOLEGARMENT MACH2XS machine, which features four needle beds. In an earlier project (PolyThread for the Cooper Hewitt Design Triennial), Sabin worked with Arup to implement an accurate stretch factor for designing with knits — testing each swatch for incremental changes to its circumference, material type, striation patterning, hole patterning, shaping for 3D seamless knit, and density, as it was loaded to the point of failure,

(2) Under the canopy

resulting in an accurate overall stretch factor of 1.5. With Lumen, further studies for smaller and larger components resulted in a more nuanced range of stretch factors, from a minimum of 1.4 to a maximum of 1.8 relative to the fully tensioned state within the net canopy. The digital knitting machines restrict the maximum relaxed circumference of each component to 48" for bulk parts and 68" for the Grove cones. The knit materials include two responsive photoluminescent yarns and a fire-retardant synthetic "fill" yarn; the former emit light and change colour after exposure to the sun or UV light.

An interactive misting system responds to human proximity, influencing the rhythm and frequency of misting. This system has three modules: electronics (with a PIR motion sensor), a control program, and solenoid valves. The control program recognizes three situations — "visitor is approaching," "no visitor," and "visitor is leaving" — each activating different instructions for the solenoid valves — from a continuous misting spray around the visitors, to a basic on and off pattern which evokes a breathing rhythm. This combination of electronics and embedded control in the misting system produces an immersive microclimate that adapts to human proximity.

Left to right: (3) Courtyard at night; (4) Night rendering of Lumen

Lumen operates at the intersection of computation, knit structures, and textile architecture, with the goals of creating responsivity, variation, and material performance. With five previous projects behind us, we felt confident that our system was ready to be pushed to the scale of the MoMA PS1 courtyards. Although Lumen was not designed as a permanent installation, it weathered summer rains and flooding and sheltered up to 7,000 people at large events. We are currently working to strengthen its weather resistance and strength, and to introduce tunable actuators in similar structures for future commissions in Abu Dhabi, Portland, and New York.

1 Project team: Concept and design: Jenny Sabin Studio; Fabrication: Shima Seiki WHOLEGARMENT, Jacobsson Carruthers and Dazian; Structural engineering: Arup; Lighting: Focus Lighting.

2 Jenny Sabin and Peter Lloyd Jones, *LabStudio: Design Research between Architecture and Biology*, London: Routledge, 2017.

3 Jenny E. Sabin, "myThread Pavilion: Generative Fabrication in Knitting Processes," *ACADIA 2013*: 347-354.

4 See Sean Ahlquist, "Social Sensory Architectures: articulating textile hybrid structures for multi-sensory responsiveness and collaborative play," *ACADIA 2015*: 263-273 and "Sensory material architectures: concepts and methodologies for spatial tectonics and tactile responsivity in knitted textile hybrid structures," *International Journal of Architectural Computing* 14, no. 1 (2016): 63-82; Mette Ramsgaard Thomsen et al, "Knit as bespoke material practice for architecture." *ACADIA 2016*: 280-289; Jane Scott, "Hierarchy in Knitted Forms: environmentally responsive textiles for architecture," *ACADIA 2013*: 361-366.

V. THE HUMAN BODY AS A METAPHOR FOR NATURE

The human body as a metaphor for nature is most readily seen in the harmony of proportion, since the body's proportions all contribute to the figure as a whole — we see this in the marble caryatids of the Erechtheion in Athens. The Roman architect Vitruvius superimposed the proportions of the human body into a square and circle, the two most perfect geometrical figures. This concept, known as *homo quadratus*, was illustrated in Leonardo da Vinci's famous drawing of Vitruvian Man, which visually conveys the modular unity of human proportion as multiples of its parts.

Bodily proportions were important to the Vitruvian concept of *symmetria*, in which the dimensions of all parts have an orderly relationship to each other. In the Baroque era, the play of deception beautifully shines in the Chinese-style mirror cabinet of Margrave Wilhelmina's Hermitage Palace in Bayreuth, where multiple mirrors deconstruct space, and the bodies in it, to create an ever-changing world of reflections and juxtapositions. Proportions related to the body find a modern life in Le Corbusier's modulor — a measurement system based on the Fibonacci series — which relates the human body to architecture, determining everything in his designs from ceiling heights to building volumes.

In the 1960s, as people saw for the first time a photograph of an astronaut floating in space, loosely tethered to his ship, our entire relationship to nature was redefined. Planet Earth was seen as finite, fragile, and beautiful. Archigram's Cushicle, a soft, fetal-like architecture, represented this newly found vulnerability. With the invention of the birth control pill, women, for the first time, could own their bodies. Ricardo Porro celebrates the feminine principle as a revolutionary art form in his design for the School of the Plastic Arts in Havana. Women designers such as Margarete Schütte-Lihotzky and Charlotte Perriand helped to redefine how the modern, liberated body moves, plays, and works in the home, redefining our living environments through furniture and equipment that is integrated into architecture.

This theme closes with "Gestures," an installation created by tracing a dancer's choreography, translating and transforming these movements to create an organic, shell-like pavilion that expresses the dynamics of motion.

MEDIEVAL ORGANICISM:
MULTILAYERED SYMBOLISM IN CLUNY III
Natalie Steele

In Christian theology, the "Body of Christ" refers not only to the body of the historical Jesus, but it also means — as the Apostle Paul used the term — the entire "body" of the Christian Church.[1] It is not surprising, then, to find in Medieval Romanesque churches the superinscription of Christ's body drawn on the plan of the building. According to Paul Naredi-Rainer, the early Christian theologian Augustine of Hippo established the connection between Christ's human form and the church building:

> [Augustine] sees an Old Testament reference to Christ as ... a model for the church, in the ark that rescued Noah and his family from the great flood. The dimensions of this ark (300 x 50 x 30 ells) symbolize the human body in whose form Christ redeemed the world: the length of the human body from the top of the head to the sole of the foot is six times the width from one side to another and ten times the depth from back to belly.[2]

This interpretation of the significance of proportion, proposed by one of the earliest church leaders, lays the foundation for the numerical symbolism that medieval builders used in designing churches. Theresa Frisch, who has studied the symbolism of churches and church ornaments, suggests that the cruciform plan can also be interpreted as Virgin, Bride, Mother, Daughter and Widow.[3] The bodily resemblance can be seen within the church layout, with the head at the chancel, hands and arms at the transepts, heart at the altar, and the rest of the body towards the West. All of these references can be found in the 12th century Abbey of Cluny III, located in Southern Burgundy, France, with an additional transept that symbolically opens the space upwards (Figure 2).[4] In the case of Cluny III, the symbolism of the cruciform plan, numbers, and proportions also connect to the Divine through the ratios of musical harmony. The proportions of Cluny III directly affect the acoustics of the Gregorian plainchant that helps to produce the sacred feeling of vastness within the church.

The dimensions recorded from studies of the remains of Cluny III suggest that the design as a whole integrated symbolic numbers as the dimensions of parts, which in Vitruvius' theory of *symmetria* have an orderly relationship with each

Left to right: (1) Distant view; (2) Axonmetric view, Cluny III

other. According to Kenneth Conant, the symbolic meaning of 100 was understood from Cyril of Alexandria as plenitude and perfection. The key dimension found in the plan is 100 feet; it is the width of the sanctuary bay containing the high altar, and multiples of 100 are used within the plan. Perfect numbers form a subset of *symmetria*; they were adapted from Vitruvius by Isidore of Seville, and applied to proportions, with the sum of the submultiples equalling the initial number in each case. For example, from within the range of 1 to 8126, only the numbers 6, 28, and 496 are perfect numbers. At Cluny III, the measurement from the centre of the apse to the back wall of the narthex is 532 feet, which is only one foot beyond the sum of the perfect numbers. As well, within the abbey several minor systems contain the symbolic medieval dimensions of seven and four.[5] Elizabeth Read Sunderland, in her study of numerical symbolism in Romanesque churches, finds that multiples of seven are often found in the measurements of the main apse, which express the "whole or completeness of anything" and the "notion of the universe." The interior heights are multiples of four, which represent the earth and four cardinal directions.[6]

The harmonious proportions of music influenced medieval buildings. Cluny III was acoustically designed for Gregorian plainchant, a melodic and rhythmic type of song initially sung in a monodic style with parallel voices.[7] As stated by Caroline van Eck, acoustic designs of the time followed mathematical ratios as an "expression of a transcendent and ideal order" and are

> connected with the pythagorean and platonic doctrine that ratios of the length of strings, which are the basis of musical harmony, are a reflection of the composition of the universe. Buildings therefore should be designed on the basis of these proportions, as a representation in stone of the divine musical harmony with which the creator has endowed the universe.[8]

The results of acoustic design based on ratios at Cluny III are shown in an archaeoacoustics study by Rafael Suárez, Alicia Alonso and Juan J. Sendra, that recorded the sound of Gregorian plainchant sung from the choir and the main altar.

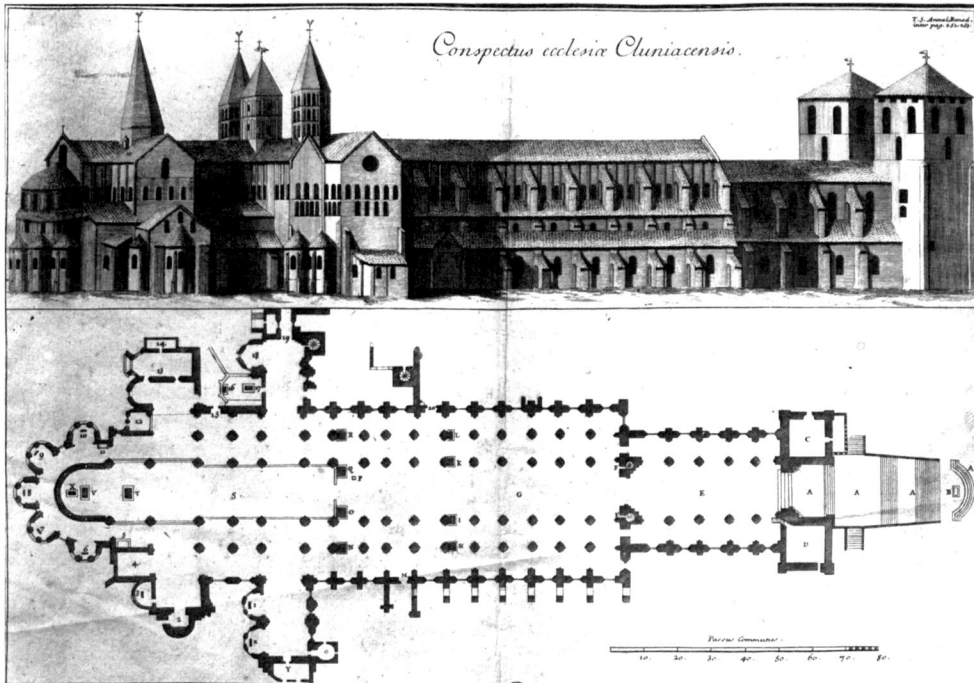

(3) Plan and longitudinal view, Church of Abbey of Cluny III. Engraving from 1754.

These results show that the song was heard clearly within the choir, but, due to a lack of sound absorption and the large volume of the church, the reverberation caused song to be unintelligible once it travelled to the central and side naves (Figure 5a).[9] The song as heard at the main altar was determined to have been complementary to that heard in the choir, because the pitch and intonation made the musical quality of the choir richer (Figure 5b). In terms of a divine experience, the reverberation of the sounds emanating from the choir and main altar enhanced one's perception of the great space of the church as a vast resonant chamber.

We have seen that organicist principles — such as the mapping of Christ's body on a cruciform plan — were practiced in Medieval ecclesiastical architecture. Also, that the architectural proportions employed in the Romanesque Cluny III were based on symbolic numbers, and these, in turn, determined the acoustic quality of the church. In monastic life, the acoustics of the church were of utmost importance, since a signficant portion of each day was spent in worship. Cluny III's choir was designed to hold 420 monks singing Gregorian plainchant. In the 12th century, it was moved from the chancel to the central nave, to accommodate the great growth of the monastic community. The sacred experience of this large choir lasted almost 200 years in Cluny III, the largest monastery in Europe.[10]

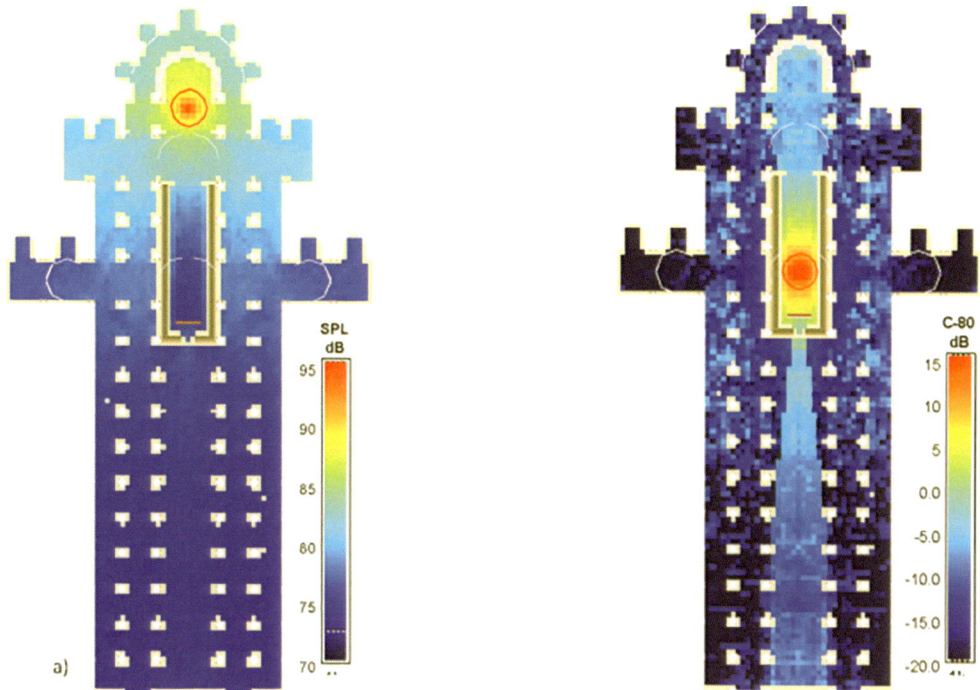

Left to right: (4a) Acoustical analysis of plainchant sung from the choir; (4b) From the main altar

1   Paul in 1 Corinthians 12:12–14 and Ephesians 4:1–16.
2   Paul von Naredi-Rainer, "Measurement and Number in Architecture," in *The Architect, the Cook and Good Taste*, eds. Petra Hagen Hodgson and Rolf Toyka. Basel: Birkhäuser, 2007, 23.
3   Teresa Frisch, "The Symbolism of Churches and Church Ornaments," *Gothic Art 1140-c. 1450: Sources and Documents*, Sources and Documents in the History of Art Series. Englewood Cliffs, NJ: Prentice-Hall, 1971, 35-36.
4   Rafael Suárez, Alicia Alonso and Juan J. Sendra, "Archaeoacoustics of Intangible Cultural Heritage: The Sound of the Maior Ecclesia of Cluny," *Journal of Cultural Heritage* 19 (2016): 5682.
5   Kenneth J. Conant, "The After-Life of Vitruvius in the Middle Ages," *Journal of the Society of Architectural Historians* 27, no. 1 (1968): 35.
6   Elizabeth Read Sunderland, "Symbolic Numbers and Romanesque Church Plans," *Journal of the Society of Architectural Historians* 18 (1959), 96.
7   Suárez et al, "Archaeoacoustics," 569.
8   Caroline van Eck, *Organicism in Nineteenth-century Architecture: An Inquiry into Its Theoretical and Philosophical Background*. Amsterdam: Architectura & Natura Press, 1994, 65.
9   Suárez et al, "Archaeoacoustics."
10   Christine Bolli, "Cluny Abbey," Khan Academy, accessed October 20, 2018, https://www. khanacademy.org/humanities/medieval-world/romanesque1/a/cluny-abbey

GENDERED LANGUAGE IN ARCHITECTURE AND ART
Karen Mills

For centuries, the human body has been used as a reference in design. Starting with Vitruvius, the connection between beauty and human proportion led to the assignment of gendered personalities to columns, thus setting up the physical vocabulary of masculine and feminine traits. In Charlotte Perriand's modern furniture design, the use of feminine and masculine words to describe design became a faux pas. Ricardo Porro represented the freedom of the Cuban people through forms representing female anatomy and the artist Yayoi Kusama uses her body as an art form to shed light on topics of gender inequality. Through examination of four different ways the female body is used both physically and symbolically in architecture and art, this essay aims to show how the use of gendered language and symbols has changed over time.

Vitruvius, writing in the first century BCE, saw that beauty in architecture was found in the proportion of the human body.[1] He drew relationships between the architecture of the body and that of buildings. He showed that his ideal human body fits within a square and circle, both considered perfect shapes. This discovery became a living rule book containing a series of laws dictated by nature. Thus, Vitruvius set the benchmark for the relationship between the body and architecture, and the way in which it is talked about.

Vitruvius considered the Classical orders to possess personalities and sexes: the Doric was considered masculine, bearing the proportion, strength and grace of a man's body; the Ionic matronly, with its feminine slenderness; and the Corinthian maidenly, bearing the the decorative accoutrements of a girl.[2] These classifications could arguably be a starting point for the gendered language often used in conversations surrounding architecture and art. In the six Caryatid columns of the Erechtheion in Athens, each female figure differs slightly, but all wear drapery which clings to the body as if it were wet, and feature a bold and dynamic positioning of their hips and legs (Figure 1).[3]

Left to right: (1) Caryatids, Erechtheion, Athens; (2) Perriand in the LC 4 *chaise longue,* Salon d'Automne, 1929. © Estate of Charlotte Perriand / SOCAN (2019)

Vitruvius' gendered language in regard to form continued into the 20th century. In 1927, Charlotte Perriand was hired by Le Corbusier to design three chairs to accommodate different body positions. The *siège à dossier basculant* (armchair with a tilting back), imagined for sitting in the living room, references Breuer's *Club Chair*, though different in scale and elaboration. The dimension suits a smaller figure, suggesting a female occupant.[4] When designing the *Chaise longue*, comfort and relaxation was the starting point. Though its designers Perriand, Le Corbusier and Pierre Jenneret also imagined a man in their descriptions of this chair, its features were often characterized using "feminine" language, such as "light" and "seductive." Mary McLeod comments that "eighteenth-century grace and eroticism have their twentieth-century equivalent in this light, undulating structure poised on four points."[5] The *chaise* was also regularly illustrated with a photograph of Perriand (Figure 2). It yet again belies the image both designers had of the chair as a representation of a lounging male body. By 1929, distinctions between male and female chair types had disappeared, as the use of tubular steel, which combines attributes then seen as both traditionally male and female, such as strength and lightness, straight lines and curves, became popular as the modern style.[6]

Unlike Perriand's chairs, which began to blur the lines between masculine and feminine, Richardo Porro's School of Plastic Arts in Havana embraced female sexuality as an inspiration for its design. Located at the entrance of the campus grounds, this complex has become the most identifiable of the five National Art Schools (Figure 3). Placing his interest in the traditions of Cuba's roots in African religion,[7] Porro wanted the architecture to express the culture and traditions of the Cuban people. Porro observes that

> Cuba is sensual. Everything touches the senses and there is nothing strange about this. It is an island bathed by the breeze, with a smooth and gentle landscape that a hand can almost caress…The fertile soil is sensual as is the walk of a Cuban woman.[8]

Left to right: (3) School of the Plastic Arts, aerial view; (4) Courtyard fountain.

These ideas about gender, femininity, and ethnicity come together in the curvilinear forms and spaces within the school, intended as expressions of female nurturing and sensuality. The pointed skylights atop the domed roofs of the studios suggest female breasts. The curved colonnaded paths are lined with arecas palms, planted specifically to look like pubic hair.[9] At the centre of the plan is Porro's most overt reference to the female body, a tiled fountain in the form a papaya, the Caribbean fruit with unmistakable sexual connotations (Figure 4). According to John Loomis, Porro's use of female imagery throughout the School of Plastic Arts demonstrates the freedom of the time, and reflects the optimism of the Cuban people during the beginning of the Revolution. For Porro, this school did not just exemplify gender, but presented the erotic nature of the tropics that allowed for open expressions of sexuality.[10]

Identity, insofar as it is defined by gender, sex, and race, often shows its presence in the body. For the artist Yayoi Kusama, the body is her canvas. She often uses it as a surface for the visual language of her personal identity, both real for her and projected by society, taken from the stereotypes she inhabits.[11] Kusama explores notions of identity and gender through various public installations, using props, make-up, wigs, and costumes. Figure 5 shows her naked body amongst phallic knobs, highlighting the juxtaposition of male symbols and female sexuality, and exposing sexual disparities.[12]

Gender finds itself in a variety of forms. Vitruvius identified that beauty was linked to human proportion. This way of thinking has been translated into the way gendered language and symbols are applied in architecture and art. Perriand, Porro, and Kusama's work each take a different approach to the use of the human body, illuminating the ways in which gendered language and symbols are constantly in flux.

(5) Yayoi Kusama, Untitled, 1966

1   Caroline van Eck, *Organicism in Nineteenth Century Architecture: an Enquiry into Its Theoretical and Philosophical Background*, Amsterdam: Architectura et Natura Press, 1994, 41.
2   John N. Summerson, *The Classical Language of Architecture*. London: Methuen, 1963, 14.
3   Mark Cartwright, "Caryatid," *Ancient History*, October 29, 2012. https://www.ancient.eu/Caryatid/.
4   Mary McLeod, "Domestic Reform and European Modern Architecture: Charlotte Perriand, Grete Lihotzky, and Elizabeth Denby," in *Modern Women: Women Artists at the Museum of Modern Art*, eds. Cornelia Butler and Alexandra Schwartz, New York: MoMA, 2010, 176.
5   McLeod, "Domestic Reform," 179-80.
6   Mary McLeod, "New Designs for Living: Domestic Equipment of Charlotte Perriand, Le Corbusier, and Pierre Jeanneret, 1928-29," in *Charlotte Perriand: An Art of Living*, ed. Mary McLeod, New York: Harry N. Abrams, 2003, 48.
7   John A. Loomis, *Cuba's Forgotten Art Schools: Revolution of Forms*, New York: Princeton Architectural Press, 1999, xxixx.
8   Loomis, *Cuba's Forgotten Art Schools*, 58.
9   Universo Rodriguez, in person tour and lecture of School of Arts, Havana, Cuba, September 27, 2018.
10 Loomis, *Cuba's Forgotten Art Schools*, 57-60.
11 Bree Richards, "Yayoi Kusama: Performing the Body," for the exhibition, *Yayoi Kusama: Look Now, See Forever* at Queensland Art Gallery, 19 November 2011 to 11 March 2012. https://play.qagoma.qld.gov.au/looknowseeforever/essays/performing-the-body/
12 Yuko Hasegawa, "Performativity in the Work of Female Japanese Artists in the 1950s-1960s and 1990s," in *Modern Women*, eds. Butler and Schwartz, 341.

LAWRENCE HALPRIN'S FOUNTAINS: A DISCOVERY OF MOVEMENT

Jamie Leer

Lawrence Halprin's (1916–2009) best-known works of landscape architecture were completed in the 1960s and '70s — the Lovejoy and Keller Fountains in Portland, Oregon and Freeway Park in Seattle, Washington. These three projects encapsulate Halprin's design theories regarding nature, process, and the body. In his essay "Nature into Landscape into Art," Halprin describes nature as "pure process made visible" and suggests "we respond to nature because we ourselves are a part of its making. We are biologically part of its creation, and therefore we empathize with the order and interrelationships in it."[1] Halprin did not intend his fountains to imitate nature, rather, he wanted them to integrate people and nature through forms inspired by natural processes.

A similar idea can be found in Caroline van Eck's book *Organicism in Nineteenth-Century Architecture*, as she reflects on the work of German architect Karl Friedrich Schinkel. Early in his career, Schinkel believed that architecture "does not follow the forms of nature in the way painting and sculpture do, but nature's 'general and fundamental laws."[2] Similarly, Halprin wrote in his notebooks "the Portland fountains are 'natural' not because they imitate nature but because the processes by which natural effects of this kind operate have been understood and recycled into an art form"[3] (Figures 1 and 2). These two statements are complementary, both suggesting that good design stems from an understanding of nature's processes rather than an imitation of its forms. This concept is established early on in van Eck's book, as a foundation for the study of organic architecture. Pursuing this insight to a study of Halprin's work allows us to view it under the lens of "organic" architecture.

Halprin was concerned with how natural processes might influence design. He was not alone in this interest — his wife, the influential modern dancer Anna Halprin, was a key collaborator in their development of a design method they called "scoring," or the RSVP Cycles (Figure 3).[4] These involved choreographing and mapping people's movements, actions, and emotions within the environment.[5]

Left to right: (1) Lovejoy fountain, 1966 (with Moore Turnbull); (2) RSVP workshop, Halprin deck, Kentfield, CA, 1968

From 1966 to 1971, the Halprins

> engaged multi-sensory activities in [various] environments according to loosely structured ... guidelines — from movement sessions, to blindfolded awareness walks, to collective building projects, to choreographed journeys in urban plazas, parks, and rail cars."[6]

Because the RSVP Cycles were developed through both dance and architecture, they were inextricably tied to the body, spatial awareness and movement. Halprin stated that "it is only when people are inside my design[s] and move through them that my design has any meaning."[7] He believed that the scores helped to achieve architectural unity between the body and its movements in space. This focus on the body in architecture extends back to Vitruvius, who wrote about the human body as being perfect in its proportions and that these proportions could serve as the basis for architectural ratios.[8]

Halprin too, took inspiration from the body and its surrounding landscape, treating them as one coherent experience. By always conceiving of the body in its surroundings, Halprin developed his large landscape features evoking waterfalls or caves in proportion to the human body, thus allowing for free-flowing movement through the designed "natural" spaces (Figure 4).[9] He also took inspiration from forms found in nature, particularly rock formations. He appreciated the sculptural qualities of rock forms eroded and shaped by water, and intuited that those forces would evoke deep desires and emotions in people.[10] This design thinking is best expressed through his fountains in Portland and Seattle.

Lawrence and Anna Halprin believed that the study of movement in space could be source of artistic inspiration. For him, "the fountain, once built, became, itself, a score for movement"[11] and he invited people to climb over them, jump into them, move and dance around in the water (Figures 5-7).[12] Anna believed that "space can be experienced most directly by movement, on a higher level, in the dance"[13] and she staged performances in his fountains to take advantage of the dynamic visual and experiential possibilities (Figure 8).

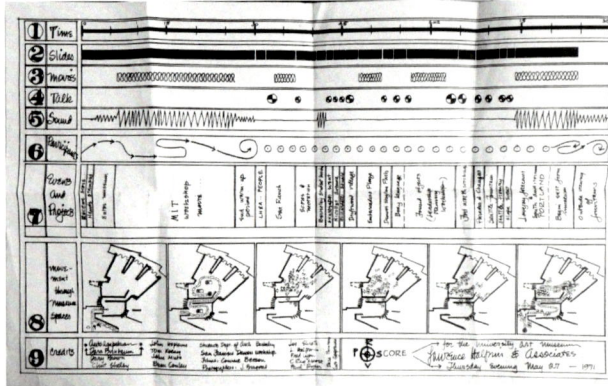

Left to right: (3) RSVP Score, University Art Museum, UC Berkeley, 1971; (4) Freeway Park, Seattle

They understood that water, a key element in all three fountains, was a "choreographic force" that stirs up the desire for movement.[14] The flow of water parallels the flow of people through the plaza, and the fountains were designed to marry these flows, so that moving bodies and flowing water form an integrated choreography. As a result, Halprin's fountains don't imitate nature's forms but rather its dynamics. Looking at photos from opening ceremonies and many performances held at the fountains, we see that the Halprins successfully merged nature and people into an experiential, and wholly new, architectural landscape.

1   Lawrence Halprin, "Nature into Landscape into Art," in *Landscape in America*, ed. George F. Thompson. Austin: University of Texas Press, 1995, 243.
2   Caroline van Eck, *Organicism in Nineteenth-Century Architecture: an Inquiry into Its Theoretical and Philosophical Background*, Amsterdam: Architectura et Natura Press, 1994, 147.
3   Lawrence Halprin, *Lawrence Halprin Notebooks, 1959-1971*. Cambridge, MA: MIT Press, 1972, 312.
4   RSVP stands for Resources, Scores, Valuaction, Performance. See Lawrence Halprin, *The RSVP Cycles: Creative Processes in the Human Environment*. New York: George Braziller, 1979.
5   Peter Merriman, "Architecture/Dance: Choreographing and Inhabiting Spaces with Anna and Lawrence Halprin," *Cultural Geographies* 17, no. 4 (October 2010): 434, doi:10.1177/1474474010376011.
6   California Historical Society, "Experiments in Environment, the Halprin Workshops, 1966-71" Exhibition (January 22-July 3, 2016). http://experiments.californiahistoricalsociety.org/exhibition/)
7   Ann E. Komara, *Lawrence Halprin's Skyline Park*, New York: Princeton Architectural Press, 2012, 28.
8   van Eck, *Organicism*, 41.
9   Halprin, "Nature into Landscape into Art," 244-247.
10 Alison Bick Hirsch, *City Choreographer: Lawrence Halprin in Urban Renewal America*. Minneapolis, MN: University of Minnesota Press, 2014, 165.
11 Hirsch, *City Choreographer*, 133.
12 Hirsch, *City Choreographer*,152.
13 Merriman, "Architecture/Dance," 433.
14 Hirsch, *City Choreographer,* 121.

Above, left to right: (5) Freeway Park, 1970s; (6) Keller Fountain on opening day; (7) Keller Fountain today
Below: (8) Dancers at Lovejoy Fountain, 1970

Portland Archives, A2012-005

BIOMETRICS IN PARTICIPATORY COLLECTIVE ART
Alan Macy

In addition to our words, we express and observe "affect" when we engage with one another. We can think of affect as the measurable aspects of an always-running body mobilization occurring within ourselves, subject to our flow of perceived experience. This mobilization can represent a myriad of physical phenomena occurring within our bodies. We make up our minds in as little as 600 milliseconds (ms). In the first 50 to 100 ms, the received sensory data from our eyes, ears and other senses begins to arrive in the vicinity of our brain. This data is still exogenous, meaning it arrives before consciousness and is subject to the neuron-channel physics of sensory perception, filtering and translation. From 100ms to 600ms, the data is processed inside the brain in the endogenous phase, activating memory and routing information subject to previous experience and developed structural frameworks. In this endogenous period, the body is oriented by incoming sensory data to mobilize as required. Affect is the consequence of this mobilization, and may involve changes in heart rate, respiratory depth, pupil diameter, skin sweating, blood pressure, blood flow and vascular resistance, among numerous other physical shifts. Affect establishes our emotional / motivational state and creates the foundation for our subsequent thoughts. An "emotion" is the label we give to the feeling of the "affect."

According to the philosopher William James, our perception of an event results in bodily changes, and our feeling of these changes is the emotion. He writes, "we feel sorry because we cry, angry because we strike, afraid because we tremble."[1] Affect is thought to manifest itself in three dimensions: arousal, motivation and valence. Arousal is a sympathetic response to stimuli; increasing arousal indicates increased activation. Motivational state indicates our inclination to act, in accordance to our perception of the act being challenging or threatening. Valence references pleasure and displeasure. In the circumplex model of arousal versus valence, where arousal is the Y axis, and valence the X axis, then motivational state could be considered the Z axis (Figure 1).[2]

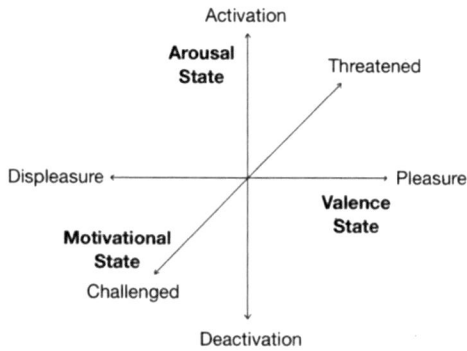

Left to right: (1) Dimensions of Affect; (2) David Rosenboom demonstrating the ARP 2500 synthesizer in the Electronic Media Lab, Department of Music, York University, Toronto, in the early 1970s.

Dimensions of Affect

Given that affect provides a foundation for our judgements, and consequently for the words we choose and the manner in which we speak them, it's reasonable to venture that affective states, and the emotion(s) they indicate, have a central role in face to face, real-time communication between people.[3] According to philosopher Martha Nussbaum, "emotions are not just the fuel that powers the psychological mechanism of a reasoning creature, they are parts, highly complex and messy parts, of this creature's reasoning itself."[4]

The idea of compositional unity, or organicism, can be considered when we speak with others face to face. Words have meanings and the way we put them together adds additional meaning.[5] Furthermore, the body language of people in conversation provides additional context — what it means, for example, when someone rolls their eyes while saying something that sounds factual.

Among the topics proposed by Caroline van Eck in her definition of architectural organicism, the idea of compositional unity emerges as a theme to develop a more focused approach for the investigative analysis of organic architecture.[6] Through Leon Batista Alberti's definition of "concinnitas," and van Eck's understanding of unity and harmony as a proponent of organic beauty, the Biometric Campfire project acknowledges unity as a type of whole which is larger than the sum of its parts.

"Biometric Campfire" follows in a line of effort, starting in the 1930s, by physiologists Edgar D. Adrian and Harold Cabot Matthews, who sonified physiological signals. Since the 1960s,

> The brain has been a focus in art-making since Alvin Lucier first unlocked the potential of Electroencephalography (EEG) in his 1965 piece "Music for Solo Performer." Lucier used the amplification of his brain waves to resonate the surface of percussion instruments, creating a scene of wonder for the audience. This work opened the field to pioneers like David Rosenboom and Richard Teitelbaum, who further contributed to the advancement and expansion of biofeedback in the arts; Rosenboom famously demonstrated EEG

music to the world in 1972 with an on air performance with John Lennon, Yoko Ono and Chuck Berry. Starting in the 1990s, artists and scientists began to develop devices better geared towards the nature of the multimodal work that artists were producing. Knapp and Lusted developed the "Biomuse" interface, a platform which acquired signals from the brain, muscles, heart, eyes, and skin. This system was notably used by biosensor pioneer Atau Tanaka. In the 2000s, the term "Brain-Computer Music Interfaces" was introduced to describe Brain-Computer Interfaces that were developed specifically for music.[7]

The Biometric Campfire is defined by the architectural space of a tensile structure designed by Filum Ltd.[8] Up to six participants sit down in a circle, around a central light column, in chairs which measure their electrocardiogram (ECG) signals. Together, the participants will craft a creative expression — it may even represent a compositional unity, where the collective outcome is larger than the sum of its parts (Figure 3).

The Biometric Campfire measures affect through the real-time collection of the heart's electrical signal, collecting data from six participants simultaneously and presenting the resulting individual and collective (averaged) data visually and in sound. The visual data is presented in a center light column, where the signals from each participant can be uniquely identified, and the column also shows the average ECG intensity occurrence for the six participants — so that it clearly reflects when the heartbeats of the group synchronize and desynchronize. The light column's intensity is further modulated by the respiratory patterns in the group, via the phenomena of respiratory sinus arrhythmia and mechanical modulation of the heart's position due to diaphragmatic breathing (Figure 4).

Simultaneously, the ECGs of the participants are directed to sound synthesis generators. Each R-wave of the ECG triggers the generation of a particular, pre-recorded sound, and each Biometric Campfire chair is assigned a different scale note produced by a zither. The timing of the note is determined by the timing of the participant's ECG and its loudness is determined by the magnitude of the R-wave. The resulting "music" is a harmony of zither notes that are struck in accordance with the occurrence and intensity of the collective heartbeats in the group.

Biometric Campfire produces a visual and auditory composition that is crafted by the emotional responses of the participants (Figure 4). It produces a result that is larger than the sum of its parts because the stimuli that drive affect, and its subsequent expression, are subject to the following phenomena:

- The music and visual display created is determined by the timing and intensity relationships between the ECG of the participants.
- The timing and intensity of the participants' ECGs are influenced by the surrounding environment, held by the architectural space, and modified by the visual and auditory stimuli present in that space.

The recursive aspect of the exhibition — in which an individual participant's affect is influenced by the group's collective, affective state or intentional creative expression —results in phenomena that could not be realized by considering the

Above: (3) Biometric Campfire
Below: (4) Diagram of Biometric Campfire as an Auditory and Visual Expression Generator

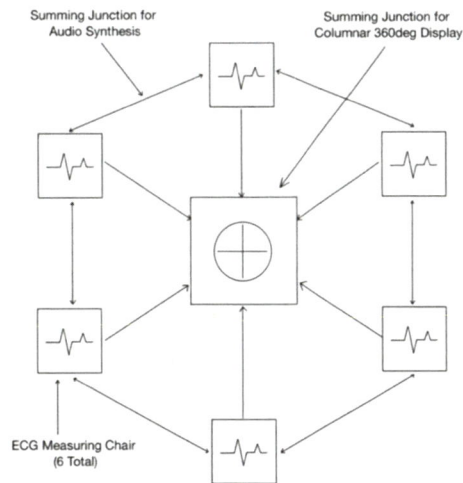

Summing Junction for
Audio Synthesis

Summing Junction for
Columnar 360deg Display

ECG Measuring Chair
(6 Total)

contributing elements in isolation.[9] This is because the expression of compositional unity contributes to the stimuli that drive the affective state of each participant. However, Biometric Campfire is simply a visceral demonstration of the realities faced when situated in any architecture. There are always the signals from individuals, that are filtered and combined by the architecture, to act as new stimuli to those same individuals.

Future Effort

This work will proceed along two paths. One direction will involve deeper evaluation of certain physiological variables. In the case of ECG (the electrical signal generated by the heart), this in-depth look will explore aspects of the signal when considering larger time intervals, such as those with many heartbeats. When considering many heartbeats in sequence, the harmonic content of the beat occurrences becomes observable. This harmonic content has a relationship to the physiological affect of the associated person. The other direction will involve multiple physiological measures to be recorded in synchrony. In this circumstance, the relationship between physiological variables, such as those generated by the heart and the lungs, can be evaluated for their interactions, both of which also relate to physiological affect.

Future iterations will also continue to involve collaboration with artists and designers to develop the auditory and visual expressions of the physiological affect. Examples of past collaborations include work with Sarah Bonnemaison's Architextiles Lab (@Lab) for the Warming Hut on the Halifax Commons (Figures 5-8); "BioRhythm," a biologically-inspired audiovisual installation with artists Ryan McGee, Yuan-Yi Fan and Rezi Ali (2011); and "Protocell Field" performance and installation, Rotterdam (2012) with architect Philip Beesley and musician Lance-David Hosale.

1   William James, "What is an Emotion?" (1884), published in *The Heart of William James*, ed. Robert Richardson, Cambridge, MA: Harvard University Press, 2012.
2   Jim Blascovich and Wendy Berry Mendes. "Challenge and threat appraisals: the role of affective cues", in J.P. Forgas (ed), *Studies in emotion and social interaction*, second series. *Feeling and thinking: The role of affect in social cognition*, New York: Cambridge University Press, 2000, 59-82.
3   Lisa Gaelick, Galen V. Bodenhausen and Robert S. Wyer, Jr., "Emotional Communication in Close Relationships," *Journal of Personality and Social Psychology* 49, no. 5 (1985): 1246-1265.
4   Martha C. Nussbaum, *Upheavals of Thought: The Intelligence of Emotions*, New York: Cambridge University Press, 2003.
5   Scott Gilbert and Sahotra Sarkar, "Embracing Complexity: Organicism for the 21st Century," *Developmental Dynamics* 219, no. 1 (2000): 1–9.
6   Caroline van Eck, *Organicism in Nineteenth-Century Architecture: an Inquiry into Its Theoretical and Philosophical Background*, Amsterdam: Architectura et Natura Press, 1994.
7   Kameron R. Christopher, Ajay Kapur, Dale A. Carnegie and Gina M. Grimshaw, "A History of Emerging Paradigms in EEG for Music," *Proceedings of the ICMA/SMC joint conference*, Athens (September) 2014.
8   The design partnership of Sarah Bonnemaison and Christine Macy.
9   Gary William Flake, *The Computational Beauty of Nature: Computer Explorations of Fractals, Chaos, Complex Systems and Adaptation*, Cambridge, MA: MIT Press, 2000.

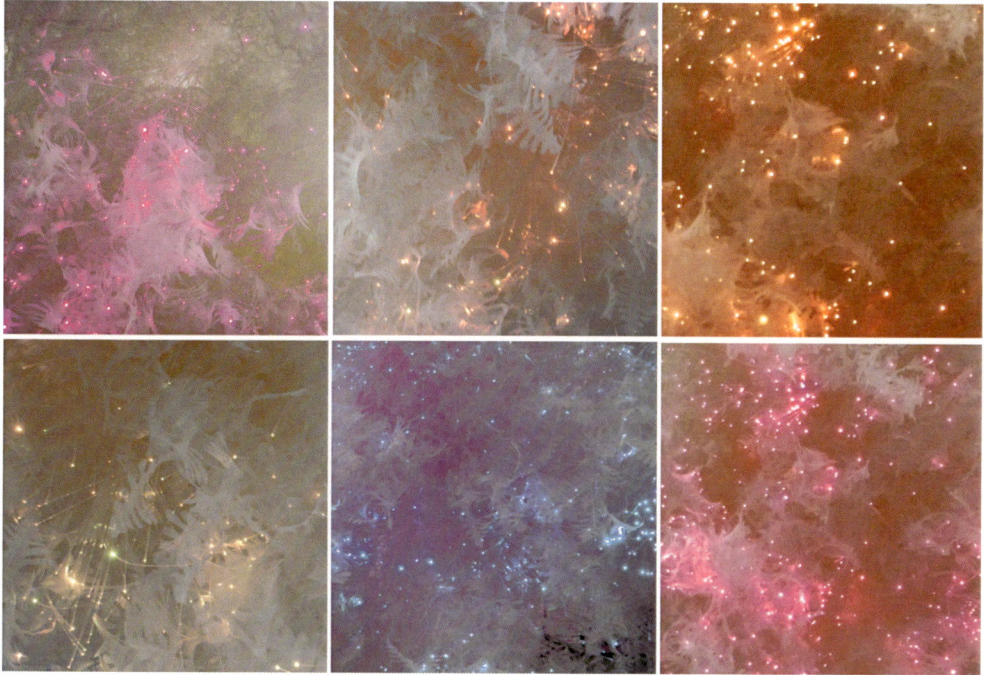

(5) Warming Hut, Halifax, 2011. Colour variations in the biometric chandelier

(6) Halifax Mayor Peter Kelly tries it out; (7) Seating circle, showing hand grip to register biometric data.

GESTURES
Filum Ltd. (Sarah Bonnemaison and Christine Macy)

One of the most persistent ways movement can be expressed is through organic forms. In fact, the idea of organic form in architecture is like a wave on the surface of the ocean — a side effect of a powerful undercurrent that has long sought to ally science and art in the discipline.

If we were to draw a thread connecting architecture that expresses ideas of movement, it would connect Baroque architecture, Art Nouveau, lightweight structures, and today's explorations with living architecture. In the Baroque era, we find perhaps the greatest examples of movement in architecture — generated by the intersection of science and art — in the pilgrimage churches of southern Germany. There, architects Balthasar Neumann and the Zimmerman brothers developed the curved volumes of these masterworks, shortly after Gottfried Leibniz published his studies of calculus in the late 17th century. The dramatic displays of movement in these churches — their tension, exuberance, grandeur, and complex curves — employed calculus to create curved geometries of the domes that attempted to approach the perfection of God's creation.

With the influence of motion studies, movement analysis became a vector for formal and spatial innovation in architecture. Examples include Lily Reich's kitchen designs for the German Exhibition in 1931; Gray's "choreographic architecture," Gerrit Rietveld's Schroeder House, Kiesler's Endless House and the Slow House by Diller and Scofidio. Art historian Georges Didi Huberman sees an essential connection between life and movement:

> The movement is the most apparent of the characters of life; it manifests itself in all functions; movement is the very essence of many of them, and in every physical notion of force, on the other

Left to right: (1) Dance: (2) Birds; (3) Traces

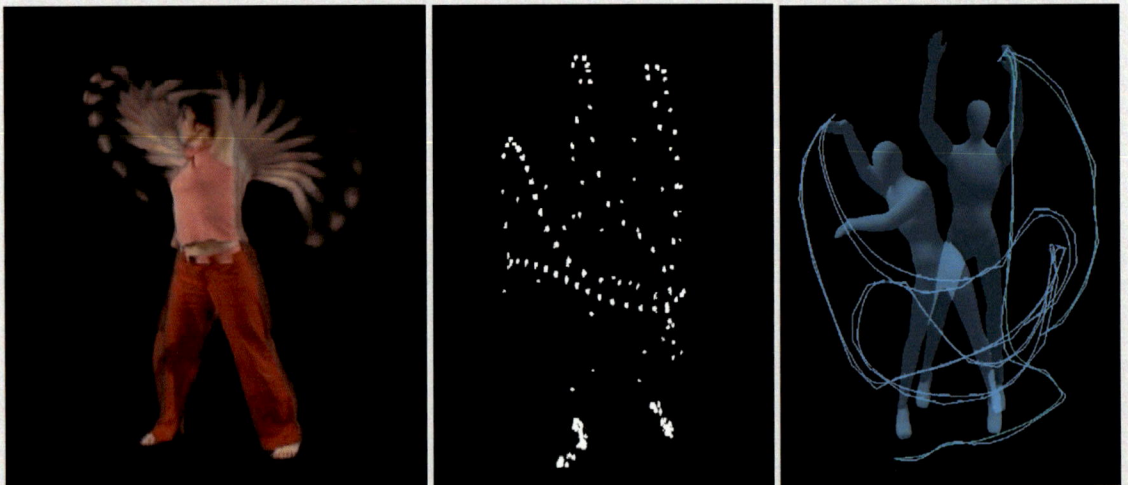

hand, tend to be reduced into one - that which engenders movement.[1]

If we were able to freeze the traces of human movement, might we envision a space of inhabitation, a "shell" or "nest" to surround the body? With this image in mind, I embarked on an exploration to create circular worlds based on the traces of movement that would shape an individual's dwelling, like a human shell.

Gestures (2006), an installation at the Maritime Museum of the Atlantic, aimed to turn movement into architecture, much in the same way that for Paul Klee, "pictorial art springs from movement, is in itself interrupted motion and is conceived as motion."[3] Our research began by videotaping activities on the Halifax waterfront that expressed the maritime culture, such as curling a rope around the cleat of a mast, a flag waving in the wind, a person pointing at a feature. Dancer Maria Osende choreographed a series of phrases that translated these everyday gestures into movements of the entire body. We recorded her choreographies using motion-capture, tracing the movement in three-dimensional digital space. The movement paths curl down into small spirals, open up into large arcs, twist into curves, and fold back on themselves.

Since "time measures motion," as Huberman remarks, "it becomes understandable that physical science, being physiological, has attempted the joined geometry of time and motion, through a graphic representation."[5] In this case, the technology of motion capture produced a graphic representation that joins the geometry of time and human motion. Thirteen points on the dancer's body were tracked in virtual space according to their x-y-z coordinates. Tracing these movements, recording them first with lines and later with stereotomic models, the dancer's movement phrase is translated into a three-dimensional graphic representation. The aim was not to create a one-to-one relationship between the motion-trace and the form — such a form would be realistic but would not express the idea of a dwelling. Traces which crisscrossed inside the sphere were removed and others were chosen to become the supporting structure of the pavilions.

Left to right: (4) Digital model: (5) Model refinement; (6) Construction

Then came the question of what materials would be used to build these human "shells." The traditional boat building of the Atlantic coast offered an array of construction techniques well adapted to complex curves. With the aid of craftsmen from the Maritime Museum, we steamed wood, bent it into curves and riveted it into place.[6] The number of layers increased to reflect the speed of the movement, its scale (a small step or a large jump), and its quality (introverted or extroverted); these variations pulsed and flowed, lending an organic feel to the movement paths.

The final step was the introduction of the tensile surfaces onto the wood framework to create an enclosure. If we think back to Leibniz, we know that the mathematical description of a curved line can be either derived or integrated — if the former, we obtain its simpler straight version, if the latter, we obtain the surface under the curve. So to generate an enclosure or dwelling, we integrated the curved lines of the wooden framework, revealing the implicit surfaces under the curves as stretched nets to create an enclosure. These tensile surfaces were developed through the form-finding process using soap-film models, each surface contributing to distribute uniform tension onto the wood members. When all the structure was complete, the forces flow evenly through the whole structure, creating its own unique equilibrium.

1 Georges Didi-Huberman et Laurent Mannoni, *Mouvements de l'air, Etienne-Jules Marey, photographe des fluids* Paris: Gallimard, 2004, 185.
2 Paul Klee quoted in Sigfried Giedeon, *Mechanization Takes Command*, New York: Oxford University Press, 1948, 109.
3 Credits for the installation *Gestures*: Architecture: Filum Ltd (Sarah Bonnemaison and Christine Macy); Dance: Maria Osende; Video: Ariella Palhke; Motion capture: Joel Dauncey NSCC Truro; Textile dying: Robin Muller.
4 Didi-Huberman, *Mouvements*, 191.
5 The construction was done by students of Dalhousie University under my supervision in a summer term design-build course. See Christine Macy, *Free Lab: Design-Build Projects from the School of Architecture, Dalhousie University, Canada, 1991-2006*, Halifax, NS: Tuns Press, 2008.

Left to right: (7) "Flag" pavilion; (8) "Rope" pavilion at night; (9) "Rope" pavilion detail. Opposite page: (10) "Rope" in the museum courtyard.

CONTRIBUTORS

PHILIP BEESLEY is a visual artist, architect, and professor at the University of Waterloo and at the European Graduate School. Beesley's work, widely cited in contemporary art and architecture, is focused on the rapidly expanding technology and culture of responsive and interactive systems. He directs the Living Architecture Systems Group and Riverside Architectural Press. His Toronto-based practice, Philip Beesley Architect Inc. [PBAI] operates in partnership with the Europe-based practice Pucher Seifert and the Waterloo-based Adaptive Systems Group, and in numerous collaborations including longstanding exchanges with couture designer Iris van Herpen and futurist Rachel Armstrong. An internationally recognized expert and pioneer in kinetic, responsive, near-living architectural installations, Beesley has exhibited his work at over 62 venues internationally, including the Biennales in Venice and Sydney, and across four continents.

SARAH BONNEMAISON is a professor in the Faculty of Architecture and Planning at Dalhousie University, Halifax. She has a doctorate in human geography from the University of British Columbia and degrees in architecture from Pratt Institute and the Massachusetts Institute of Technology. As an architect, she specialized in lightweight structures and practiced in offices in Germany and in the US before starting her office Filum Ltd, in collaboration with Christine Macy. Sarah is also a writer — her books include *Architecture and Nature*; *Festival Architecture*; *Installations by Architects*; and *Responsive Environments*, as well as numerous contributions to edited volumes and journals. Her passion lies in bringing history and theory to life through interactive exhibitions and installations for performance. Her current research explores notions of the organic in architectural theory and practice.

CAROLE COLLET is Professor in Design for Sustainable Futures at Central Saint Martins, University of the Arts London where she currently holds two key roles. As CSM-LVMH Director of Sustainable Innovation, she set up Maison/0, an incubator of creative sustainable innovation, in partnership with the luxury group LVMH. She is also Director of the Design & Living Systems Lab, a research lab which explores the interface of biological sciences and design to propose new sustainable models of biofabrication. As an educator, she has pioneered the integration of sustainability in the curriculum by establishing the MA Textile Futures in 2001 and the first MA in Biodesign in 2018. In her research, Collet questions the emerging role of the designer when working with biological systems. She established an original framework for sustainable biodesign, first published with the inaugural curation of 'Alive, New Design Frontiers' in 2013. Her work has been featured in international exhibitions and she regularly contributes to conferences on the subjects of biodesign, biomimicry, and sustainable futures.

BRIAN LILLEY is an architect and professor of Architecture at Dalhousie University, with interests in ecological, artistic, and computational strategies for design. As a partner at sauerbruch hutton architects, he focused on ecological design and assemblies, particularly the sensored double-façade for the GSW Headquarters project in Berlin; in Canada, he collaborated with Richard Kroeker on a Health Center for the Pictou Landing First Nation. A member of Dalhousie's Institute for Research in Materials, Lilley works with Aaron Outhwaite and Rory MacDonald to advance cross-disciplinary research in ceramic materials, in Smart Geometry workshops and Dalhousie's design-build Freelabs. In 2017, he was awarded a Lieutenant Governor's award and a Halifax Urban Design Award (with FBM Architects) for the design of the Hope Blooms greenhouse. His recent project, developed with the Narratives in Space + Time Society — "Walking the Debris Field: Public Geographies of the Halifax Explosion, 2014-2017" — focuses on augmented environments to develop knowledge-enhanced forms of mobility that enrich the human experience.

ALAN MACY is the R&D Director, past President and a founder of BIOPAC Systems, Inc. He designs data collection and analysis systems used by researchers in the life sciences, that help identify meaningful interpretations from signals produced by life processes. Trained in electrical engineering and physiology, with over 30 years of product development experience, he is currently focusing on psycho-physiology, emotional and motivational state measurements, magnetic resonance imaging and augmented/virtual reality implementations. He presents in the areas of human-computer interfaces, electrophysiology, and telecommunications. His recent research and artistic efforts explore ideas of human nervous system extension and the associated impacts upon perception. As an applied science artist, he specializes in the creation of cybernated art, interactive sculpture, and environments.

STEVEN MANNELL is an architect, professor of Architecture, and founding Director of Dalhousie's College of Sustainability. His research focuses on 20th century waterworks and the conservation of modern built heritage. He is curator and author of *Atlantic Modern: The Architecture of the Atlantic Provinces 1950-2000* (2001), and *"Living Lightly on the Earth:" Building an Ark for Prince Edward Island 1974-76* (2018), which considers the Ark in the context of 20th century counterculture, the Appropriate Technology movement, and the emergence of "ecological architecture."

JENNY SABIN is the founder of Jenny Sabin Studio, an experimental architectural design studio based in Ithaca, and Director of the Sabin Design Lab at Cornell AAP, a trans-disciplinary design research lab with specialization in computational design, data visualization, and digital fabrication. In 2006, Sabin co-founded the Sabin+Jones LabStudio, a hybrid research and design unit, together with biologist Peter Lloyd Jones. She is also a founding member of the Nonlinear Systems Organization, a research group started by Cecil Balmond at PennDesign, where she was Senior Researcher and Director of Research. Sabin's collaborative research, including bioinspired adaptive materials and 3D geometric assemblies, has been funded by the National Science Foundation and the private sector, including Nike Inc., Microsoft Research, Autodesk, the Cooper Hewitt Smithsonian Design Museum, MoMA, the Centre Pompidou, the Museum of Craft and Design, and the Exploratorium.

FURTHER READING

Abalos, Iñaki, Renata Snetkiewicz, and Lluís Ortega. *Abalos Sentkiewicz: Essays on Thermodynamics, Architecture and Beauty*. New York: Actar D, 2015.

Ballantyne, Andrew. "The Unit of Survival", *ARQ* 20, no. 1 (March 2016): 39-44.

Beesley, Philip and Sarah Bonnemaison, eds. *On Growth and Form: Organic Architecture and Beyond*, Halifax: Tuns Press, 2008.

Belier, Corinne, Barry Bergdoll and Marc Le Coeur. *Henri Labrouste: Structure Brought to Light*. New York: MoMA, 2012.

Borden, Gail P. and Michael Meredith, eds. *Matter: material processes in architectural production*. New York: Routledge, 2012.

Bud, Robert. *The Uses of Life: a History of Biotechnology*. Cambridge: Cambridge University Press, 1993.

Constant, Caroline and Wilfried Wang, eds. *Eileen Gray: An architecture for all the senses*. Frankfurt am Main and Cambridge MA: Deutsches Architekturmuseum and Harvard University Graduate School of Design, 1996

Dessauce, Marc. "Eileen Gray, Villa E1027: une contribution a l'histoire de l'architecture orga-nique en France," *Bulletin de la societé de l'histoire de l'art Francais* (1988): 233-244.

Di Palma, Vittoria. "Architecture and the organic metaphor," *The Journal of Architecture* 11, no. 4 (2006), 385-390.

Fathy, Hassan. *Natural Energy and Vernacular Architecture*. Chicago: University of Chicago Press, 1986.

Flake, Gary William, *The Computational Beauty of Nature: Computer Explorations of Fractals, Chaos, Complex Systems and Adaptation*, Cambridge, MA: MIT Press, 2000.

Gans, Deborah and Zehra Kuz, eds. *The Organic Approach to Architecture*. London: Wiley-Academy, 2003.

Giedeon, Sigfried. *Mechanization Takes Command*. New York: Oxford University Press, 1948.

Gilbert, Scott, and Sahotra Sarkar. "Embracing Complexity: Organicism for the 21st Century," *Developmental Dynamics* 219, no. 1 (2000): 1–9.

Hallam, Elizabeth and Tim Ingold, eds. *Making and Growing: Anthropological Studies of Organ-isms and Artefacts*. London: Routledge, 2016

Hvattum, Mari "'Unfolding from Within': Modern Architecture and the Dream of Organic Totality," *The Journal of Architecture* 11, no. 4, 2006: 497-509.

Ingraham, Catherine T. *Architecture, Animal, Human, the Asymmetrical Condition*. New York and London: Routledge, 2006.

James, Kathleen. "Expression, Relativity, and the Einstein Tower," *Journal of the Society of Architectural Historians* 53, no. 4 (December), 1994: 392-413.

Laugier, Marc Antoine. *Essai sur l'Architecture*, 1755.

Le Corbusier. *The Modulor and Modulor 2*. London: Faber and Faber. 1954.

Lesaffre, Micheline, Pieter-Jan Maes, Marc Leman, eds. *The Routledge Companion to Embodied Music Interaction*, London: Routledge, 2017.

Loomis, John A. *Cuba's Forgotten Art Schools: Revolution of Forms*. New York: Princeton Press, 1999

Macy, Christine and Sarah Bonnemaison. *Architecture and Nature: Creating the American Landscape*. London and New York: Routledge, 2003.

Mannell, Steven. *Living Lightly on the Earth: Building an Ark for Prince Edward Island 1974-76*. Halifax, NS: Dalhousie Architectural Press, 2018.

McLeod, Mary, ed. *Charlotte Perriand: An Art of Living*. New York: Harry N. Abrams, 2003, 36-67.

Menges, Axel. *Frei Otto, Bodo Rasch: Finding Form, Towards an Architecture of the Minimal*. Deutscher Werkbund Bayern, 1995.

Mertins, Detlef. "Where architecture meets biology: an interview with Detlef Mertins," in *Interact or die!* eds. Jole Brouwer and Arjen Mulder, Rotterdam: V2 Publishing, 2007.

Minke, Gernot. *Building with Earth, Design and Technology of a Sustainable Architecture*. Berlin: Birkhäuser Publishers for Architecture, 2006.

Moe, Kiel. *Insulating Modernism: Isolated and Non-Isolated Thermodynamics in Architecture*. Basel: Birkhauser, 2014.

Nitschke, Günter. "From Shinto to Ando," *Studies in Architectural Anthropology in Japan*, London: Academy Press, 1993.

Noboru, Kawazoe. *Ise: Prototype of Japanese Architecture*, Cambridge, MA: MIT Press, 1965.

Pawlyn, Michael. *Biomimicry in Architecture* (2nd ed). Newcastle: RIBA, 2016.

Payne, Alina. *From Ornament to Object: Genealogies of Architectural Modernism.* New Haven, CT: Yale University Press, 2012.

Rawes, Peg ed. *Relational Architectural Ecologies: Architecture Nature and Subjectivity*. Lon-don: Routledge, 2013.

Sabin, Jenny and Peter Lloyd Jones, *LabStudio: Design Research between Architecture and Biology*, London: Routledge, 2017.

Sergeant, John. *Frank Lloyd Wright's Usonian Houses: The Case for Organic Architecture*. New York: Whitney Library of Design, 1976.

Summerson, John N. *The Classical Language of Architecture*. London: Methuen, 1963.

Tavernor, Robert William, *Concinnitas in the architectural theory and practice of Leon Battista Alberti* (Doctoral thesis, University of Cambridge), 1985.

Terranova, Charissa and Meridith Tromble, eds. *Routledge Companion to Biology, Art and Architecture*. London and New York: Routledge, 2016.

Thompson, D'Arcy W. *On Growth and Form*. Cambridge: Cambridge University Press, 1917.

van Eck, Caroline. "Organicism revisited. The desire for the animation of the inanimate matter in the 19th century", *Archithese* 43, no. 4 (2013): 52-58.

van Eck, Caroline. *Organicism in Nineteenth Century Architecture, an enquiry into its theoretical and philosophical background*. Amsterdam: Architectura et Natura Press, 1994.

Wright, Frank Lloyd. *Organic Architecture*. Cheshire: Lund Humphries, 1939.

Wright, Frank Lloyd, and Meehan, Patrick Joseph. *Truth against the World: Frank Lloyd Wright Speaks for an Organic Architecture*. New York and Toronto: Wiley, 1987.

Zevi, Bruno. *Towards an Organic Architecture*, London: Faber and Faber, 1950.

ILLUSTRATION CREDITS

Cover to page vi:

Cover: Jenny Sabin Studio. *Introduction:* Photo by Fabrizio Pivari, 2017 [CC BY-SA 4.0]

Pages 1-25

Introduction: Photograph by David Iliff, 2007 [CC BY-SA 3.0]. *Godden:* (1) Photograph by Livioandronico2013, 2016 [CC BY-SA 4.0]; (2) Photograph by Ursus, 2012 [CC BY-SA 3.0]; (3) Photograph by Josep Renalias [CC BY-SA 3.0]. *Fransen:* (1) Drawing by Christine Macy, using HABS ILL,16-OAKPA,3-; (2) Photograph by QuartierLatin1968 [CC BY-SA 3.0]; (3) Photograph by Raphael Azevedo Franca [Public Domain] via Wikimedia Commons; (4) Photograph by James Steakley [CC BY-SA 4.0]; (5) https://en.wikiarquitectura.com/building/herbert-jacobs-house-1/. *Khan:* (1) https://www.japansociety.org.uk/event/the-ise-shrines/; (2) Photograph by 663highland, 2008 [CC BY-SA 3.0]; (3) https://www.the-saleroom.com/en-gb/auction-catalogues/lacy-scott-and-knight/catalogue-id-srlac10128/lot-e73271cb-2830-4705-8270-a52b00f1ba24; (4) © Kiyonori Kikutake; (5) Photograph by "yusunkwon from Cambridge, Massachusetts", 2007 [CC BY-2.0]; (6) Photograph by Chris73 [CC BY-SA 3.0], from Wikimedia Commons. *PB/LASG:* (1-4, 7-8) IMage by Philip Beesley/LASG; (5) Photograph by Yannis Vlamos; (6) Photo by Luk~commonswiki [CC BY-SA 4.0], from Wikimedia Commons.

Pages 26-49

Introduction: Photograph by Dartmouth College Electron D21Microscope Facility, 2004 [Public Domain] via Wikimedia Commons. *Vandergeest:* (1) National Gallery of Art, Washington, DC, Photograph by Sailko, 2009 [CC BY-SA 3.0]; (2) Public domain, Photograph by Luc Viatour, 2007; (3) Alberti, with additional information by Gaurav Gangwar; (4) User: Coldrerio [CC BY-SA 3.0]; (5) Photograph by RAF, 1944 [Public Domain] via Wikimedia Commons. *Follett:* (1) Photograph by Eino Mäkinen, Alvar Aalto Museum. 1939; (2) Photograph by Maija Holma, Alvar Aalto Museum; (3) Photograph by Martti Kappanen, Alvar Aalto Museum; (4) Photograph by Gustav Welin, Alvar Aalto Museum; (5) Photograph by Michele Merckling, Alvar Aalto Museum; (6) Photograph by Asko Salokorpi, Museum of Finnish Architecture. *Maclean:* (1-5) © Ibuku. *Adnan:* (1-5) Courtesy of the Heritage Foundation of Pakistan. *Brian Lilley:* (1-5, 8-10) Photograph by Brian Lilley; (6) Drawing by Brian Lilley; (7) Wikimedia Commons.

Pages 50-73

Introduction: © Photograph by Mansour Sedaghat, National Spiritual Assembly of the Bahá'ís of Chile *Turnbull:* (1) Unknown author [CC0] via Wikimedia Commons; (2) Étienne-Louis Boullée [Public domain]; (3) Not stated [Public domain] via Wikimedia Commons; (4) Photograph NASA/Bill Anders [Public Domain]; (5) © Larry Keenan; (6) Archives Nationale du Quebec, fonds "Armour Landry" P97, P13447. *Mannell:* (1-2, 4) Solsearch Architects; (3, 5) Patrick Lefebvre. *Landry:* (1) Dwight Lathrop Elmendorf [Public domain] via Wikimedia Commons; (2) National Archives, NARA 519832 [Public domain]; (3) Passivhaus Institut derivative work by Michka B [CC BY-SA 3.0]; (4-7) © KPMB, 2008. *Falls:* (1, 3) © Philippe Rahm architectes, Mosbach paysagistes, Ricky Liu & Associates; (2) Toupiewakou [CC BY-SA 4.0]; (4) Norbert Aepli, Switzerland [CC BY 2.5]. *Logan:* (1) Unknown author; (2) Photo by Stevekeiretsu [CC BY-1.0]; (3) Dartmouth College Electron Microscope Facility; (4) Photograph by Jürgen Matern, 2006 [CC BY-SA 2.5]; (5) © Grimshaw Architects. *Carole Collet:* (1-3) © Carole Collet.